American ENGLISH FILE 3

Workbook

Christina Latham-Koenig
Clive Oxenden
Jane Hudson

Paul Seligson and Clive Oxenden are the original co-authors of
English File 1 and *English File 2*

OXFORD
UNIVERSITY PRESS

Contents

1
- 4   **A**   Mood food
- 7   **B**   Family life
- 10   **PRACTICAL ENGLISH** *Meeting the parents*

2
- 11   **A**   Spend or save?
- 14   **B**   Changing lives

3
- 17   **A**   Race across Florida
- 20   **B**   Stereotypes – or are they?
- 23   **PRACTICAL ENGLISH** *A difficult celebrity*

4
- 24   **A**   Failure and success
- 27   **B**   Modern manners?

5
- 30   **A**   Sports superstitions
- 33   **B**   Love at Exit 19
- 36   **PRACTICAL ENGLISH** *Old friends*

6
- 37   **A**   Shot on location
- 40   **B**   Judging by appearances

7
- 43   **A**   Extraordinary school for boys
- 46   **B**   Ideal home
- 49   **PRACTICAL ENGLISH** *Boys' night out*

8
- 50   **A**   Sell and tell
- 53   **B**   What's the right job for you?

9
- 56   **A**   Lucky encounters
- 59   **B**   Too much information!
- 62   **PRACTICAL ENGLISH** *Unexpected events*

10
- 63   **A**   Modern icons
- 66   **B**   Two crime stories
- 69   **LISTENING**

ONLINE SELF-ASSESSMENT MATERIAL

Powerful listening and interactive practice

The American English File Second Edition Download Center includes class audio, workbook audio, all video, and a Progress Check for each File.

- **AUDIO** – Download ALL of the audio files for the Listening and Pronunciation activities in this Workbook for on-the-go listening practice.
- **PRACTICE** – Check your progress by taking a self-assessment test after you complete each File.

AUDIO

When you see this symbol ONLINE, go to www.oup.com/elt/americanenglishfile:

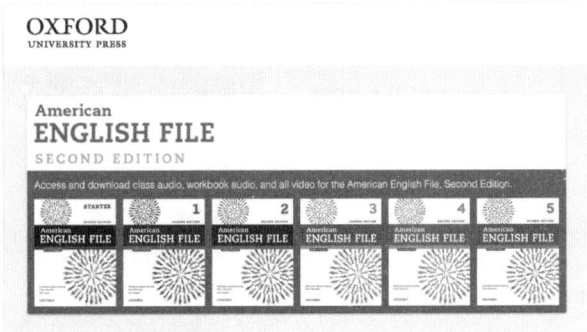

Choose the correct level or American English File.

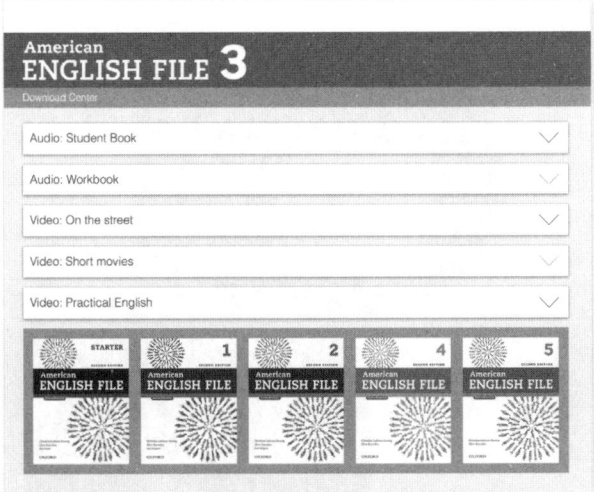

Choose "**Audio: Workbook**."

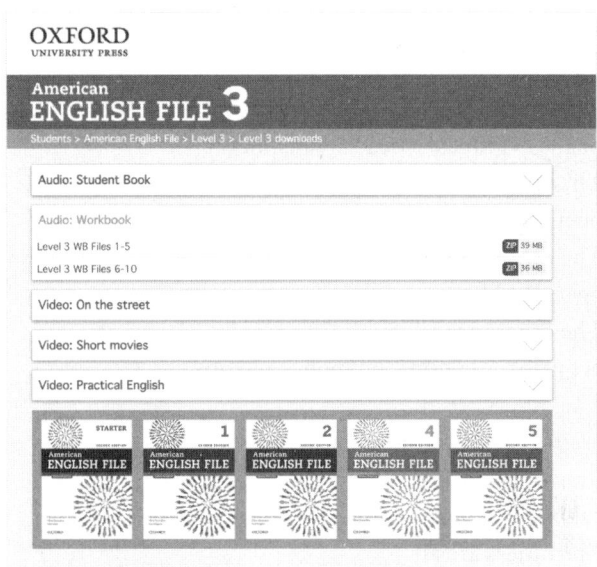

PRACTICE

At the end of every File, there is a Progress Check.

To do the Progress Check, select the File you have just finished.

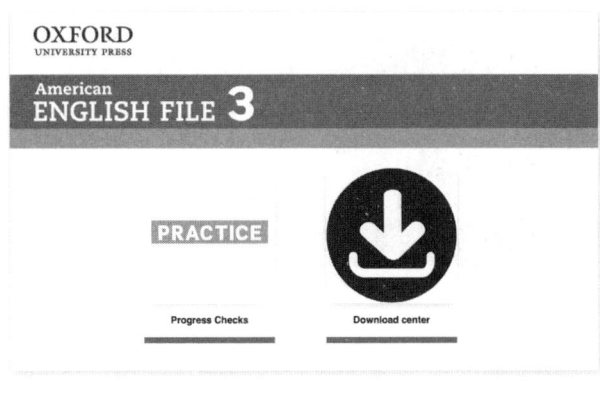

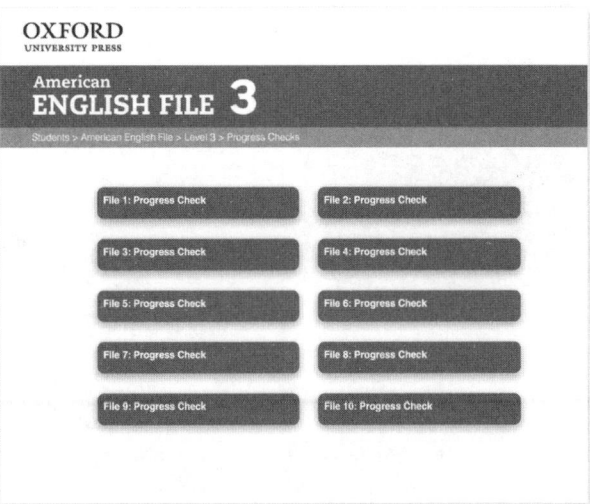

> The two biggest best-sellers in any bookstore are the cookbooks and the diet books.
> The cookbooks tell you how to prepare the food and the diet books tell you how not to eat any of it.
>
> Andy Rooney, US humorist

1A Mood food

1 VOCABULARY food and cooking

a Circle the word that is different. Explain why.

1 **beans** grapes peach raspberry
  The others are all ___fruit___.
2 beef pork lamb salmon
  The others are all _____.
3 beet cabbage pear pepper
  The others are all _____.
4 eggplant lemon mango melon
  The others are all _____.
5 crab mussels beef shrimp
  The others are all _____.
6 cabbage cherry zucchini cucumber
  The others are all _____.

b Complete the crossword.

c Complete the sentences with the words in the box.

~~canned~~ fresh frozen low-fat raw spicy take-out

1 ___Canned___ tomatoes usually last for about two years.
2 I don't feel like cooking. Let's get _____ for dinner.
3 Are there any _____ peas in the freezer?
4 I'm don't really like _____ fish, so I never eat sushi.
5 Hannah's on a diet, so she bought some _____ yogurt to have for dessert.
6 They eat a lot of _____ food in Mexico.
7 We buy _____ bread from the bakery every morning.

Clues down ↓

Clues across →

1 G R I L L E D

2 PRONUNCIATION vowel sounds

a Write the words in the chart.

beef carton chicken chocolate cook crab
soup jar mango peach raw salt
sausage squid sugar tuna

1 fish	2 tree	3 cat	4 car
	beef		

5 clock	6 saw	7 bull	8 boot

b **ONLINE** Listen and check. Then listen again and repeat the words.

Pronouncing difficult words

c Write the words.
1 /bɔɪld/ — boiled
2 /ˈkæbɪdʒ/ — _____
3 /ˈspaɪsi/ — _____
4 /ˈroʊstɪd/ — _____
5 /ɡreɪps/ — _____
6 /frut/ — _____
7 /beɪkt/ — _____
8 /ˈmɛlən/ — _____
9 /zuˈkini/ — _____

d **ONLINE** Listen and check. Then listen again and repeat the words.

3 GRAMMAR simple present / continuous, action and nonaction verbs

a Are the highlighted phrases right (✓) or wrong (✗)? Correct the wrong phrases.

1 Does your girlfriend like seafood? ✓
_____
2 Lucy's in the kitchen. She makes a cup of coffee. ✗
She's making
3 Are you eating out every weekend? ☐
_____
4 I don't know what to cook for dinner. ☐
_____
5 Are you thinking the fish is cooked now? ☐
_____
6 We're having lunch with my parents every Sunday. ☐
_____
7 My mother's in the yard. She's mowing the lawn. ☐
_____
8 I'm not wanting any potatoes with my fish, thanks. ☐
_____
9 Do you prefer steamed rice to fried rice? ☐
_____
10 Jack's on the phone. He orders some pizzas. ☐
_____

b Complete the sentences with the simple present or continuous form of the verbs in parentheses.

1 Our neighbors _grow_ all of their own vegetables. (grow)
2 My mother _____ usually _____ on the weekend. (not cook)
3 Do you want to come for lunch on Sunday? We _____ roast chicken. (have)
4 We _____ tonight because there's a soccer game on TV. (not go out)
5 _____ you usually _____ your birthday with your family? (spend)
6 That restaurant _____ delicious mussels at lunchtime. (serve)
7 How often _____ you _____ in a typical week? (eat out)
8 I _____ an appetizer because I'm not hungry. (not have)
9 We _____ often _____ steak. (not buy)
10 My boyfriend's on a diet so he _____ on fried food. (cut down)

4 READING

a Read the article once and put the headings in the correct place.

A Can I eat apples?
B How can I prevent serious illnesses?
C How should I start the day?
D Do I really need to eat five a day?

The truth about healthy eating

Food experts are always telling us what we should and shouldn't eat, but they often give us different advice. Our food writer, Teresa Gold, has taken a look at all the information to figure out what is fact and what is fiction.

1 _C_
A typical American breakfast of fried eggs, bacon, toast, pancakes, and orange juice will certainly stop you from feeling hungry, but it's high in calories, which means that you'll gain weight if you eat it regularly. A healthier option is to have just an egg. Boil it instead of frying it, and eat it with a piece of toast made with whole-wheat bread. Breakfast cereals are very high in sugar, so if you feel like cereal, have granola – with no added sugar. You can also get your first vitamins of the day by drinking a glass of freshly squeezed orange juice.

2 _____
Fruits and vegetables contain the vitamins and minerals we need to stay healthy. But five is actually a fictional number thought up by an American nutritionist. She looked at what the average person ate and doubled it. According to more recent research, the right number is actually eight. The research shows that people who have eight pieces of fruit and vegetables a day are much less likely to suffer from heart disease than those who eat three.

3 _____
This particular fruit has had some bad publicity because dentists say it can harm our teeth. While it's true that apples do contain a little sugar, they are also a source of fiber. Nutritionists say that we need about 18 grams of fiber a day, and a medium apple – peel included – contains about 3 grams. Some varieties contain more fiber than others, so you should choose carefully.

4 _____
The key to good health is a balanced diet that contains fats and carbohydrates as well as proteins, vitamins, and minerals. Fats may be high in calories, but they also contain vitamins. According to the World Cancer Research Fund, you should only have about 500 grams of red meat per week – a steak is about 100 grams. One type of food on its own won't kill or cure you, but eating the right amount of the right food will stop you from getting sick.

b Read the article again. Mark the sentences T (true) or F (false).

1 A typical American breakfast every morning isn't good for you. _T_
2 The best breakfast is any type of cereal. ___
3 An American nutritionist carefully calculated the amount of fruits and vegetables we should eat. ___
4 We should eat more than five servings of fruits and vegetables per day. ___
5 Apples contain a lot of sugar. ___
6 All apples have the same amount of fiber. ___
7 Fats can be good for us. ___
8 You can eat as much red meat as you want to. ___

c Look at the highlighted words and phrases. What do you think they mean? Use your dictionary to look up their meaning and pronunciation.

5 LISTENING

a ONLINE Listen to a radio call-in program about the article in exercise **4**. Check (✓) the caller(s) who completely agree with it.

A Kevin ☐   C Derek ☐
B Kate ☐   D Rosie ☐

b Listen again and answer the questions.
Which caller…?
1 thinks that some fruits and vegetables are unhealthy ___
2 says that most children prefer fast food ___
3 eats very little fruit ___
4 is very healthy because he/she eats a lot of fruits and vegetables ___

c Listen again with the audioscript on p. 69.

USEFUL WORDS AND PHRASES

Learn these words and phrases.

carbohydrates /kɑrboʊˈhaɪdreɪts/
protein /ˈproʊtin/
awake /əˈweɪk/
oily /ˈɔɪli/
powerful /ˈpaʊərfl/
relaxed /rɪˈlækst/
sleepy /ˈslipi/
stressful /ˈstrɛsfl/
beneficial /bɛnəˈfɪʃl/
ready-made food /ˌrɛdi meɪd ˈfud/

> Happy families are all alike; every unhappy family
> is unhappy in its own way.
> *First line of* **Anna Karenina** *by Leo Tolstoy, Russian writer*

1B Family life

1 GRAMMAR future forms

a Complete the sentences with the correct form of the verbs or phrases on the right.

1 My brother hates his job. *He's going to look for* a new one. **he / look for** (an intention)
2 Don't worry about the drinks. _____ for them. **I / pay** (an offer)
3 _____ some more coffee. **I / make** (an offer)
4 Do you think _____ before you're 30? **you / get married** (a prediction)
5 _____ to my cousin's wedding. We'll be on vacation. **we / not go** (an arrangement)
6 A Are you ready to order?
  B Yes, _____ the steak. **I / have** (an instant decision)
7 _____ 21 on my next birthday. **I / be** (a fact)
8 _____ for dinner tonight. You paid last time. **we / pay** (an offer)
9 I'm going to the mall. _____ long. **I / not be** (a promise)
10 _____ a party for my grandmother's 80th birthday tomorrow. **we / have** (an arrangement)

b Complete the dialogues with the correct future form of the verbs in parentheses.

1 A *Are* you *going away* this weekend? (go away)
  B No, we _____ here. Why? (stay)
  A We _____ a barbecue. Would you like to come? (have)

2 A I'm too tired to cook. I _____ some Chinese take-out food tonight. (order)
  B Good idea. I _____ the restaurant. What do you want for an appetizer? (call)
  A I _____ the spring rolls, please. (have)

3 A What time _____ you _____ in the morning? (leave)
  B I _____ the six o'clock train. (take)
  A I _____ you a ride to the train station. (give)

4 A What _____ you _____ tonight? (do)
  B I _____ the new James Bond movie. Do you want to come? (see)
  A No, thanks. I've already seen it. You _____ it! (love)

5 A I _____ you with the dishes. (help)
  B OK. I _____ and you can dry. But please be careful with the glasses. (wash)
  A Don't worry. I _____ anything! (not break)

2 each other

Rewrite the sentences with *each other*.

1. My brother's shouting at my sister and she's shouting at him.
   My brother and sister _are shouting at each other_.
2. Rob doesn't know Alex and Alex doesn't know Rob.
   Rob and Alex _____.
3. I'm not speaking to my sister and she isn't speaking to me.
   My sister and I _____.
4. I don't understand you and you don't understand me.
   We _____.
5. The coach respects the players and they respect him.
   The coach and the players _____.

3 PRONUNCIATION sentence stress

a **ONLINE** Listen and complete the sentences.

1. _When_ are you going to _book_ your _vacation_?
2. I'm _____ going to _____ the _____ yet.
3. I'm going to _____ _____.
4. _____ are you _____ _____?
5. I'm _____ some _____.
6. I'm _____ _____ my _____.
7. _____ will you _____ your test _____?
8. I _____ get them _____ _____.
9. I'll _____ them on _____.

b Listen again and repeat. Copy the rhythm.

4 VOCABULARY family, adjectives of personality

a Complete the sentences with a family word.

1. Your mother and father are your p_arents_.
2. Your grandfather's father is your gr_____-gr_____.
3. A child who has no brothers or sisters is an on_____ ch_____.
4. Your brother's daughter is your n_____.
5. Your father's sister is your a_____.
6. Your spouse, children, parents, and brothers and sisters are your im_____ f_____.
7. Your father's new wife is your s_____.
8. Your wife's or husband's father is your f_____-i_____-l_____.
9. Your aunts, uncles and cousins are your ex_____ f_____.
10. Your brother's or sister's son is your n_____.

b Match the comments with the personality adjectives in the box.

aggressive ambitious independent
jealous reliable self-confident selfish
sensible ~~spoiled~~ stubborn

1. "When I want something, my parents always give it to me."
   spoiled
2. "I don't like my boyfriend talking to other women."
   _____
3. "I'm always there when my friends need my help."
   _____
4. "Those are my pens and you can't borrow them."
   _____
5. "I'm going to go to bed early so I can sleep well before my test tomorrow."
   _____
6. "I'll hit you if you do that again!"
   _____
7. "I feel very comfortable when I'm speaking in public."
   _____
8. "I'd like to be the manager of a big multinational company."
   _____
9. "That's what I think and I'm not going to change my mind."
   _____
10. "I'd prefer to do this on my own, thanks."
    _____

c Write the opposite adjectives. Use a negative prefix if necessary.

1. generous — _cheap_
2. kind — _____
3. lazy — _____
4. mature — _____
5. organized — _____
6. sensitive — _____
7. talkative — _____
8. clean — _____

5 READING

a Read the article once. Why do the Bedouins prefer to live together in a big family group?

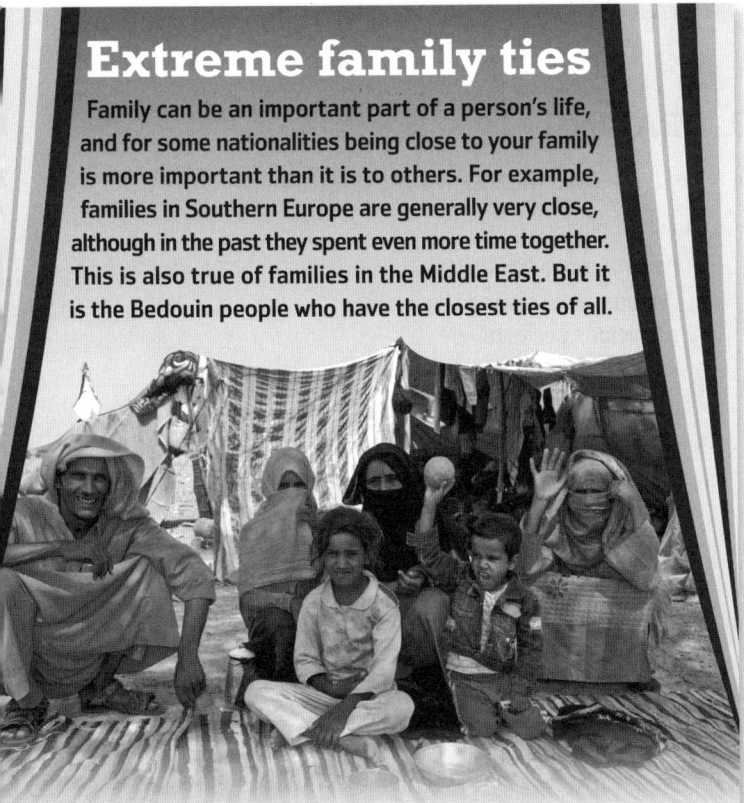

Extreme family ties

Family can be an important part of a person's life, and for some nationalities being close to your family is more important than it is to others. For example, families in Southern Europe are generally very close, although in the past they spent even more time together. This is also true of families in the Middle East. But it is the Bedouin people who have the closest ties of all.

Traditional Bedouin families live in large tents about half the size of a basketball court. The tents are divided into two sections: the first is for receiving guests in true Bedouin style – they have the reputation of being the world's most generous hosts. Visitors are always served a big meal as soon as they arrive. The second part of the tent is the family's shared kitchen, living room, dining room, and bedroom. They don't have tables and chairs, as the whole family sits on the floor to eat. And instead of beds, everybody sleeps on mattresses, which are piled into a corner of the room during the day.

Several generations usually share the tent. The head of the family is the mother, and she is the one who gives the orders. Her husband and her children live with her, even when the children are married and have their own children. The sons and sons-in-law look after the animals, while the daughters and daughters-in-law clean the tent, cook the meals, and take care of the younger grandchildren. The older ones are left to run around outside. There may often be as many as 30 people under the same roof.

The few young people who have left the family to live in the city visit their mothers nearly every day. It can be quite a surprise to see a shiny new Mercedes pull up outside one of the tents and watch a well-dressed man get out to greet his relatives.

Bedouin people do not like to be separated from their families and there is a very good reason why. If they are poor, sick, old, or unemployed, it is the family that supports them. Elderly people are never left alone, and problems are always shared. Children who work in the city are often responsible for their families financially. In this way, Bedouin families aren't just close; they are a lifeline.

b Read the article again. Choose the correct answers according to the information given.

1 In the past, most families in Southern Europe and the Middle East were…
   a smaller.   (b) closer.   c richer.
2 There isn't much … in a Bedouin tent.
   a furniture   b light   c space
3 Bedouin … spend most of the day inside.
   a men   b women   c children
4 Young Bedouins who live in the city…
   a hardly ever go home.
   b don't earn much money.
   c don't lose touch with their families.
5 Members of a Bedouin family help each other to…
   a survive.   b get a job.   c choose clothes.

c Look at the highlighted words and phrases. What do you think they mean? Use your dictionary to look up their meaning and pronunciation.

6 LISTENING

a **ONLINE** Listen to a couple, Terry and Jane, talking about going to live with the in-laws. What do they decide at the end of the conversation?

b Listen again and mark the sentences T (true) or F (false).

1 Terry and Jane are both very tired. _T_
2 Terry is more optimistic about the future than Jane. __
3 Terry's parents have suggested the family move in with them. __
4 Terry says that if they all lived together, his parents would babysit. __
5 Jane thinks that the new plan would mean less housework for her. __
6 Jane worries that the grandparents would spoil the children. __

c Listen again with the audioscript on p. 69.

USEFUL WORDS AND PHRASES

Learn these words and phrases.

boarding school /ˈbɔrdɪŋ skul/
childhood /ˈtʃaɪldhʊd/
gang /gæŋ/
gathering /ˈgæðərɪŋ/
rivalry /ˈraɪvəlri/
sick /sɪk/
value /ˈvælyu/
fight /faɪt/
aware of /əˈwɛr əv/
no wonder /noʊ ˈwʌndər/

ONLINE FILE 1

Practical English Meeting the parents

1 REACTING TO WHAT PEOPLE SAY

Complete the dialogues.

1	Ben	Oh, ¹ n_o_! I don't ² b_____ it!
	Charlotte	What's wrong!
	Ben	I didn't tell my mom that you don't eat meat.
	Charlotte	You're ³ k_____!
	Ben	No, I'm not. Never ⁴ m_____. I'll tell her now.
		Mom! Charlotte's a vegetarian.
	Mom	⁵ R_____?
	Charlotte	Yes, but it isn't a problem.
	Mom	What a ⁶ p_____! I made a meat lasagna. But there's plenty of salad.
	Charlotte	That's fine. Thanks, Mrs. Lord.
2	Steve	We have something to tell you. We found a house that we like.
	Jill	⁷ H_____ fantastic!
	Steve	And it isn't too expensive.
	Jill	That's great ⁸ n_____! Could I see it some time?
	Steve	⁹ W_____ a great idea! I'll call and make an appointment.

2 SOCIAL ENGLISH

Complete the dialogues with the phrases in the box.

a really nice guy   Go ahead   How do you see   I mean
How incredible   Not really   That's because   things like that

1 A What did you think of my dad?
  B He's _a really nice guy_.
2 A _____ your future?
  B I think we'll be very happy together.
3 A I hear you speak Spanish. Are you bilingual?
  B _____. But I can speak it well.
4 A I'm sorry. I'm not very hungry.
  B _____ you ate too much for lunch!
5 A You know, I think we went to the same school.
  B _____!
6 A Can I have another piece of chicken, please?
  B _____. There's more in the kitchen.
7 A What kind of books do you read?
  B Biographies, history books, _____.
8 A You wouldn't want to go to the concert with us.
  B Yes, I would! _____, I love classical music.

3 READING

a Read the text and answer the questions.

In which place…?

1 can you see a celebrity — _Café Carlyle_
2 do musicians come to hear other musicians perform — _____
3 can you hear international styles of jazz — _____
4 can you see what's happening online — _____
5 should you buy a ticket before you go — _____
6 does the music finish very late — _____

Jazz in New York

New York is famous for its jazz, and for music fans no trip to the city is complete without a visit to one of the many jazz venues. Here are four of the many places you can go to hear jazz being performed.

Barbès
Barbès is a bar and performance venue in the Park Slope neighborhood of Brooklyn. Come here to listen to musical styles from all over the world, such as Mexican, Lebanese, Romanian, and Venezuelan along with traditional American styles. Usually $10 to get in.

55 Bar
Located in Greenwich Village, this small club, which started in 1919, has a very interesting history. Come to hear jazz guitarists play, and expect to see lots of serious jazz fans and music students from local colleges and music schools. Usually $10–20.

Smalls
This club was created in 1994, but has already become very famous in New York because well-known players such as Norah Jones began their careers here. The club closed in 2002, but opened again in 2004, with a more comfortable room and a website that features live streaming video of all performances. It opens from 4 p.m. to 4 a.m. $20 to get in.

Café Carlyle
Come to the first floor of the famous Carlyle Hotel to visit the Café Carlyle. It's particularly worth going on Monday nights – not only will you hear jazz from the Eddy Davis New Orleans Jazz Band, but you will also hear the famous movie director Woody Allen play with them. As well as being a director, Woody Allen is also a jazz musician. Sets at 8:45. The venue holds only 90 and is often sold out, so it's a good idea to book ahead. But it isn't cheap – tickets start at $100.

b Underline five words or phrases you don't know. Use your dictionary to look up their meaning and pronunciation.

> When a man tells you he got rich through hard work, ask him: Whose?
>
> Don Marquis, US Writer

2A Spend or save?

1 VOCABULARY money

a Complete the sentences with the correct verb in parentheses.

1. My sister __wastes__ a lot of money on clothes she never wears. (wastes / saves)
2. I can't _____ to buy a house of my own. (pay / afford)
3. You'll have to _____ a lot of money if you want to travel around the world next year. (cost / save)
4. Kevin _____ about $2,500 a month at his new job. (wins / earns)
5. That painting _____ a lot of money. (charges / is worth)
6. My uncle is doing a bike ride to _____ money for charity. (raise / save)
7. We still _____ the bank a lot of money. (owe / earn)
8. Mary _____ $5,000 from her grandfather when he died. (inherited / invested)
9. The plumber _____ me $250 to fix my shower. (cost / charged)
10. Can you _____ me $200 until I get paid? (borrow / lend)

b Complete the sentences with the correct preposition.

1. I'll pay __for__ the movie tickets if you get the snacks!
2. They charged us $5 _____ a bottle of water.
3. They got _____ debt when they bought their new house.
4. We borrowed some money _____ my parents.
5. My grandparents always pay _____ cash.
6. I don't mind lending money _____ family.
7. They spent a lot of money _____ their son's education.
8. Can I pay _____ credit card?
9. Phil invested all his money _____ his own company.

c Complete the advertisement with the words in the box.

ATM ~~bank account~~ bills coin loan mortgage salary taxes

What's so good about CASH Internet Banking plc

OUR ACCOUNT SERVICES

Open a [1] __bank account__ with us and we'll give you a free gift – you'll get a tablet computer if you earn over $3,000 a month. Consult our online service 24/7 and use your card in the [2] _____ of any bank to take out as much or as little money as you want. Do you have a lot of change? Use our free [3] _____ counter and deposit the total directly into your savings account. Does your company pay your [4] _____ directly into the bank? Then we won't charge you anything for your card. We'll even pay all your [5] _____ for you, free of charge.

OUR FINANCING SERVICES

Do you need to borrow money for a car, a vacation, or a new laptop? We'll give you a [6] _____ of up to $10,000 for whatever you want to buy.

And how about a new house? We can give you a [7] _____ at one of the lowest interest rates on the market.

OUR EXTRA SERVICES

How much do you pay in [8] _____? Talk to our specialists to make sure you're paying the right amount – they can help you pay less.

Come to CASH Internet for the best accounts, the best services, and the best savings.

11

2 PRONUNCIATION the letter o

a Circle the word with a different sound.

1 up	2 clock	3 phone	4 horse	5 bird
m**o**ney	h**o**nest	d**o**ne	aff**o**rd	w**o**rk
n**o**thing	sh**o**pping	**o**we	w**o**rse	w**o**rld
~~s**o**ld~~	d**o**llar	g**o**	st**o**re	sh**o**rt
w**o**n	cl**o**thes	l**o**an	m**o**rtgage	w**o**rth

b ONLINE Listen and check. Then listen again and repeat the words.

3 GRAMMAR present perfect and simple past

a Circle the correct answer.
1. I *have never owed* / *never owed* any money to the bank in my life.
2. They *have charged* / *charged* us too much for our meal last night.
3. I know some great cheap places to stay in Seoul. *I've been* / *I went* there a few times.
4. Paul *hasn't inherited* / *didn't inherit* anything from his grandmother when she died.
5. *You've lent* / *you lent* him money so many times, but he never pays you back!
6. How much *has your TV cost* / *did your TV cost*?
7. How many times *have you wasted* / *did you waste* money on clothes you never wear?
8. I *haven't had* / *didn't have* any coins, so I couldn't put any money in the parking meter.
9. *Have you ever invested* / *Did you ever invest* any money in a company?
10. My girlfriend has a high-paying job. She *has earned* / *earned* $85,000 last year.

b Complete the dialogues with the correct form of the verbs in parentheses.

1. **A** When ___did___ your son ___buy___ his car? (buy)
   B When he _____ his driving test last month. (pass)
2. **A** How much money _____ you _____ from your sister yesterday? (borrow)
   B About $100, but I already _____ it all. (spend)
3. **A** _____ you _____ a new house yet? (find)
   B Yes, and the bank _____ to give me a mortgage. (agree)
4. **A** _____ you ever _____ any money to a friend? (lend)
   B Only to my boyfriend when he _____ a new phone. (need)
5. **A** _____ your mother _____ an appointment with the doctor yet? (make)
   B Yes, she _____ him yesterday and she's seeing him tomorrow. (call)

4 READING

a Read the first chapter of a book about Daniel Suelo once. Where did he decide to live?

1. with friends ☐
2. with family ☐
3. in the country ☐
4. in a city ☐

The man who quit money

In the first year of the twenty-first century, a man standing by a busy road in the middle of the United States took his life savings out of his pocket – $30 – laid it inside a phone booth, and walked away. He was 39 years old, came from a good family, and had been to college. He was not mentally ill, nor did he have any problems with drugs or alcohol. The decision was made by a man who knew exactly what he was doing.

In the twelve years since then, as the stock market has risen and fallen, Daniel Suelo has not earned, received, or spent a single dollar. In an era when anyone who could sign his name could get a mortgage, Suelo did not apply for loans. As public debt rose to eight, ten, and finally thirteen trillion dollars, he did not pay taxes, or accept any type of help from the government.

Instead he went to live in a cave in Utah, where he picks fruit and wild onions, collects animals that have been killed on the road, takes old food that has gone past its sell-by date out of trash cans, and is often fed by friends and strangers. "My philosophy is to use only what is freely given or discarded," he writes. While the rest of us try to deal with taxes, mortgages, retirement plans, and bank accounts, Suelo no longer even has an ID card.

Daniel is not a typical tramp. He often works – but refuses to be paid. Although he lives in a cave, he is extremely social, remains close to friends and family, and has discussions with strangers on his website which he checks at the local library. He has ridden his bike long distances, traveled on freight trains, hitchhiked through nearly every state in the United States, worked on a fishing boat, collected mussels from Pacific beaches, caught salmon in streams in Alaska, and spent three months living in a tree after a storm.

"I know it's possible to live with zero money," Suelo declares. And he says you can live well.

b   Read the chapter again and choose the correct answers.

1   What do we learn about the man in the first paragraph?
    a   He had just left school.
    (b) He had thought about his actions carefully.
    c   He had had a difficult childhood.
2   What has Daniel Suelo done since he changed his life?
    a   He has gotten into debt.
    b   He has bought a house.
    c   He hasn't used any money.
3   How does he get enough to eat?
    a   He finds food.
    b   His family cooks for him.
    c   He buys food.
4   What's Daniel Suelo like?
    a   He's shy.
    b   He's lazy.
    c   He's outgoing.
5   How does he get from one place to another?
    a   He rides his bike everywhere.
    b   He uses different methods of transportation.
    c   He always uses trains.

c   Look at the highlighted words and phrases. What do you think they mean? Use your dictionary to look up their meaning and pronunciation.

d   Complete the sentences with one of the highlighted words or phrases.

1   Clean fresh water often comes from mountain _streams_.
2   It's important to have a _____ _____ for when you get old.
3   The giant fish sculptures in Rio were made using _____ plastic bottles.
4   The early nineteenth century was an important _____ for opera.
5   He has shares in some companies, so he's interested in what happens on the _____ _____.
6   You might get sick if you eat food after its _____-_____ _____.

5 LISTENING

a   **ONLINE** Listen to four speakers talking about how they manage on their incomes. Match the speakers with their situation.

Speaker 1   _d_   a   a single parent
Speaker 2   __   b   a family with children
Speaker 3   __   c   a single retired person on a pension
Speaker 4   __   d   a young person who lives with his / her parents

b   Listen again and mark the sentences T (true) or F (false).

Speaker 1
1   He doesn't earn much money.   _F_
2   He saves most of his salary.   __
Speaker 2
3   She doesn't own the house where she lives.   __
4   She thinks money is more important than family.   __
Speaker 3
5   He can't live on his income.   __
6   He isn't in debt.   __
Speaker 4
7   She only works in a store on the weekends.   __
8   She spends most of her money on her children.   __

c   Listen again with the audioscript on p. 69.

USEFUL WORDS AND PHRASES

Learn these words and phrases.

backer /ˈbækər/
billionaire /ˈbɪlyənɛr/
brand /brænd/
customer /ˈkʌstəmər/
entrepreneurial /ˌɑntrəprəˈnəriəl/
low-paying /loʊ ˈpeɪɪŋ/
rejection /rɪˈdʒɛkʃn/
salesman /ˈseɪlzmən/
self-made /sɛlfˈmeɪd/
wealthy /ˈwɛlθi/

2B Changing lives

> Only I can change my life. No one else can do it for me.
> *Carol Burnett, US actress & comedian*

1 GRAMMAR present perfect simple + *for* / *since*; present perfect continuous

a Write the words and phrases in the box in the correct column.

> 2005 a long time a week March six months
> I was little the last two days Tuesday
> years and years you last called

for	since
	2005

b Complete the sentences with the present perfect form of the verb in parentheses and *for* or *since*.

1. *I've had* my car *for* about a month. (have)
2. My mom _____ sick _____ last Friday. (be)
3. We _____ each other _____ we were in school. (know)
4. He _____ for the same company _____ five years. (work)
5. They _____ in Miami _____ they got married. (live)
6. My parents _____ away _____ for three days. (be)
7. I _____ to go to Australia _____ a long time. (want)
8. She _____ to me _____ last year. (not speak)

c Complete the dialogues with the present perfect continuous form of the verbs.

1. **A** Have you heard Heather's new band?
   B No. *Have they been playing* together for a long time? (they / play)

2. **A** How long was your flight?
   B Twelve hours. _____ all day. (we / travel)

3. **A** My brother has a very good job in New York City.
   B Really? How long _____ there? (he / work)

4. **A** Diana finally found a new apartment!
   B Oh good! _____ one for so long! (she / look for)

5. **A** Why does Eric's teacher want to see you?
   B _____ his homework lately. (he / not do)

6. **A** You're late.
   B Yes, I know. Sorry. _____ long? (you / wait)

7. **A** You look exhausted.
   B _____ the kids all day! (I / take care of)

d Circle the correct form. If both forms are possible, check (✓) the sentence.

1. How long *have you lived* / *have you been living* abroad? ✓
2. *I've studied* / *I've been studying* Chinese for two years.
3. Hannah *has had* / *has been having* the same boyfriend since she was in school.
4. How long *has Mark played* / *has Mark been playing* the bass guitar?
5. *He's worked* / *He's been working* at this school since he started teaching.
6. *I've known* / *I've been knowing* you for years.
7. *We've gone* / *We've been going* to the same dentist since we were kids.
8. *You've worn* / *You've been wearing* that coat for years!

2 PRONUNCIATION sentence stress

a **ONLINE** Listen and complete the sentences.
1. I've been __traveling__ all __day__.
2. How _____ have they been going _____ together?
3. She's been _____ sick since _____.
4. They _____ been _____ here for long.
5. We've been _____ the house all _____.
6. I _____ been _____ well lately.

b Listen again and repeat the sentences. <u>Copy</u> the <u>rhythm</u>.

3 READING

a Read the article once and match photos 1–3 with paragraphs A–C.

b Read the article again. Answer the questions with the letters A, B, or C.

Which organization…?
1. takes people for two weeks or a month __B__
2. encourages sightseeing ___
3. offers accommodations in tents ___
4. says what volunteers should bring ___
5. gives volunteers free afternoons ___
6. lets volunteers stay with others in a hut ___
7. arranges accommodations with local people ___
8. only needs volunteers for part of the year ___

c Look at the highlighted words and phrases. What do you think they mean? Check with your dictionary.

d Complete the sentences with one of the highlighted words or phrases.
1. My little niece only wants to play on the ___swing___ when we go to the park.
2. If you all _____ _____ _____, we'll be able to buy our colleague a nice going-away present.
3. I'd rather see animals in _____ than in a zoo.
4. The school is organizing an after-school club for _____ children in the area.
5. The people waiting for the buses were standing underneath the _____ because it was raining.
6. We're moving to a new house this weekend. Can you come and _____ _____ _____ with the packing?

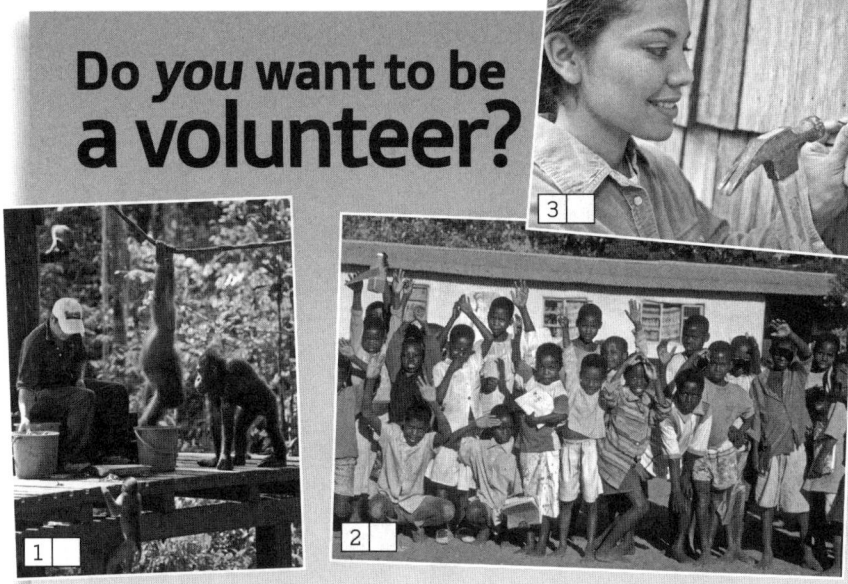

Do *you* want to be a volunteer?

A The Book Bus
Do you enjoy reading? Do you like children? Then why not volunteer for our mobile library service in Zambia? We work with underprivileged children in public elementary schools, and it's a lot of fun. We read stories, do art projects, and organize activities to help the children learn English. After breakfast at 7 a.m., we head to our first school in time for the beginning of the school day. Every morning we visit at least four schools, and we spend about an hour in each one. We get back to our campsite at around 2 p.m. for lunch, and after that you have the afternoon free to relax or prepare activities. The project takes place from May to September, and it's open to everyone. Volunteers have to pay for their own flight and make a contribution to the project.

B The Great Orangutan Project
Are you an animal lover? If you are, then you should come to Kubah National Park in Borneo. We need people to help us take care of our orangutans. Unfortunately, you won't be able to touch the animals because they are being prepared to be released into the wild, but you'll work very close to them. You'll spend your time in the Wildlife Center repairing the shelters where the orangutans live, or building new ones. You might have to make a swing, or install some ropes where the animals can play. You'll share a room in a wooden hut that looks out onto the rainforest. The program lasts for two or four weeks and it costs $1,935 or $2,820 respectively, excluding flights.

C Construction in Peru
Are you good at making things? If you are, and you'd like to take part in a construction project, how about coming to Peru to lend a hand? You'll be based in Cuzco in southeastern Peru, and you'll be involved in the construction of a small school, and a community center or an orphanage. You may have to paint and make repairs to existing buildings, or build new ones in and around the city. You'll live with a Peruvian family, and you'll eat all your meals together in their house. All of the houses have electricity and running water, but you'll have to go to an Internet cafe in Cuzco if you want to go online. You are expected to work from Monday to Friday, and on the weekends you can explore some of the fantastic sights in the region. Please bring your own work clothes.

4 VOCABULARY strong adjectives

a Complete the adjective for each picture.

1 She's absolutely fr<u>eezing</u>.

2 It's d_____!

3 They're really e_____.

4 He's h_____.

5 It's absolutely en_____.

6 They're f_____.

b Complete the sentences with a strong adjective.

1 **A** Are you **sure** the meeting is today?
   B Yes, I'm absolutely _positive_.
2 **A** Is your boyfriend's apartment **small**?
   B Yes, it's really _____.
3 **A** Were your parents **angry** about your test scores?
   B Yes, they were _____.
4 **A** Is your sister **afraid** of insects?
   B Yes, she's absolutely _____ of them.
5 **A** Were you **surprised** when you passed your driving test?
   B Yes, I was really _____.
6 **A** Were the kids **hungry** when they arrived?
   B Yes, they were absolutely _____.

5 LISTENING

a **ONLINE** Listen to a news story about an American family who is traveling around the world doing volunteer work. Check (✓) the places they have already visited.

1 Australia ✓
2 Antarctica ☐
3 China ☐
4 Haiti ☐
5 India ☐
6 Kenya ☐
7 Paraguay ☐
8 Peru ☐
9 Russia ☐
10 Rwanda ☐
11 Thailand ☐
12 Zanzibar ☐

b Listen again and answer the questions.

1 What did J.D. Lewis use to do?
   He used to be an actor.
2 How old are the children?
   _____.
3 How much is the trip going to cost?
   _____.
4 What's the name of his organization?
   _____.
5 What did they do in Thailand?
   _____.
6 How did they help the children in Rwanda?
   _____.
7 Who did they help in Kenya?
   _____.
8 What does J. D. Lewis hope his organization will do in the future?
   _____.

c Listen again with the audioscript on p. 70.

USEFUL WORDS AND PHRASES

Learn these words and phrases.

blisters /ˈblɪstərz/
charity /ˈtʃærəti/
kayak /ˈkaɪæk/
ache /eɪk/
target /ˈtɑrgət/
melt /mɛlt/
paddle /ˈpædl/
risky /ˈrɪski/
go forward /goʊ ˈfɔrwərd/
sponsor projects /ˈspɑnsər ˈprɑdʒɛkts/

ONLINE FILE 2

3A Race across Florida

A good traveler has no fixed plans.
Lao Tzu, Taoist Philosopher

1 VOCABULARY transportation

a Complete the crossword.

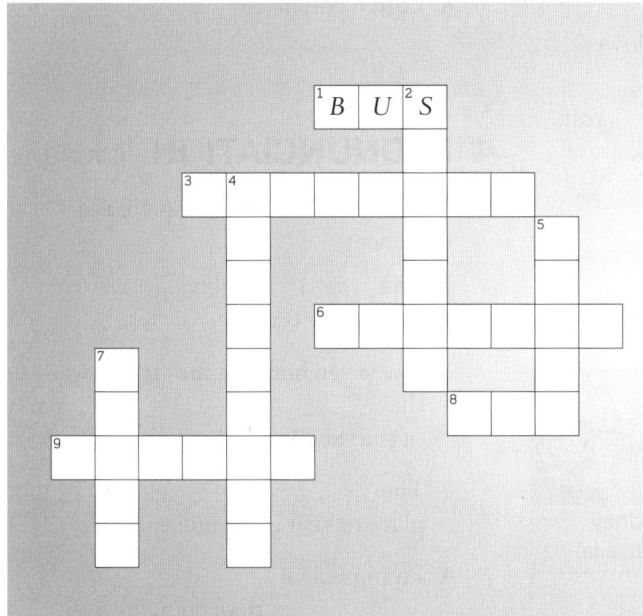

Clues across →
1 It's a large vehicle that carries passengers and stops regularly to let them on and off.
3 It's where you wait for a train at a train station.
6 It's a fast road where traffic can travel long distances between large towns or cities.
8 It's bigger than a car but smaller than a truck.
9 It's a type of railway system that travels under the ground.

Clues down ↓
2 It's a like a motorcycle but less powerful.
4 It's a type of small train that moves by electricity along special rails.
5 It's very long and used for transporting people or things by rail.
7 It's used for transporting large quantities of things by road.

b Complete the compound nouns with one word.
1 Don't forget to put your _seat_ belt on.
2 You'll get a _____ ticket if you leave your car there.
3 Sorry we're late. We were stuck in a _____ jam downtown.
4 We got held up by the _____ work on the freeway.
5 I wish bike riders would use the _____ lane instead of the sidewalk.
6 We need to fill up at the _____ station before we leave.
7 Traffic is always worse during _____ hour.
8 There aren't any cabs waiting at the _____ stand.
9 Slow down! There are _____ cameras on this road.
10 We stopped at the _____ light and waited for it to turn green.

2 PRONUNCIATION /ʃ/, /dʒ/, and /tʃ/

a (Circle) the word with a different sound.

1 /dʒ/ jazz	2 /ʃ/ shower	3 /dʒ/ jazz	4 /tʃ/ chess
dan**g**erous bri**dge** (**r**u**sh**)	**cr**ash **s**eat belt **st**ation	**ch**eck-in pa**ss**enger traffic **j**am	**ch**emistry **c**at**ch** depar**t**ure

b ONLINE Listen and check. Then listen again and repeat the words.

3 GRAMMAR comparatives and superlatives

a Complete the sentences with one word.
1. Gas isn't as expensive in the US __as__ it is in the UK.
2. My father drives more slowly _____ my mother.
3. They said that today was _____ hottest day of the year.
4. Let's go by train. It's _____ comfortable than the bus.
5. This is the _____ flight I've ever been on. I'll never fly with this airline again.
6. I think trains are _____ dangerous than cars. There are fewer accidents.
7. It's _____ to go by subway than by bus. Buses are much slower.
8. The 405 is the _____ crowded freeway in California.
9. You're at the Sheraton? We're staying at the same hotel _____ you.
10. Why don't we ride our bikes? It's the _____ expensive way to travel.

b Write sentences with the information from the survey. Use the comparative or the superlative.

Where to go?
We reveal the results from our reader survey of three popular vacation destinations.

	Cancun (Mexico)	Beijing (China)	Sydney (Australia)
It's cheap.	●●●	●●	●
It's crowded.	●	●●●	●●
It's easy to get to.	●●	●●●	●
It's exciting.	●●●	●●	●●
It's hot.	●●●	●	●●●
It's relaxing.	●●	●	●●●

1. Cancun / cheap / Beijing
   Cancun is cheaper than Beijing.
2. Beijing / crowded / of the three destinations
   _____.
3. Beijing / easy to get to / Sydney
   _____.
4. Sydney / exciting / Cancun
   _____.
5. Sydney / hot / Beijing
   _____.
6. Sydney / relaxing / of the three destinations
   _____.

c Rewrite the comparative sentences in b using (not) as … as.
1. **expensive** (sentence 1)
   Cancun isn't as expensive as Beijing.
2. **difficult** (sentence 3)
   _____
3. **exciting** (sentence 4)
   _____
4. **cold** (sentence 5)
   _____

4 PRONUNCIATION linking

a **ONLINE** Listen and complete the sentences.
1. The __most__ __relaxing__ way to travel is by train.
2. The seven hours in the airport was the _____ _____ part of the vacation.
3. The _____ _____ place to visit is the museum.
4. Flying is a lot _____ _____ than going by bus.
5. They should have the party at their house. It's much bigger _____ _____.
6. Scooters aren't _____ _____ _____ motorcycles.

b Listen again and repeat the sentences. Listen carefully to the linked words. Copy the rhythm.

5 READING

a Read the article once. Which is the oldest form of transportation?

Unusual ways of getting around

Bamboo trains
This is the best way to see rural Cambodia. A bamboo train, or *nori* as the locals call it, is a bamboo platform on wheels that travels along tracks. It's powered by an engine, and it can reach a speed of 25 miles per hour. Passengers sit on a grass mat on the nori. Noris may not be as comfortable as conventional trains, but they're certainly a lot cheaper. Pick up a nori from Battambang Station, but remember to agree on a price before you get on.

Totora reed boats

These boats have been around for centuries. They are made from the reeds that grow on the banks of Lake Titicaca, one of the largest lakes in South America. As well as making boats from totora reeds, the local people use them to make their houses, which they build on floating islands. Totora reed boats are still used for hunting and fishing, but today some of the local people transport people across the lake in them. Traveling on a reed boat among the floating islands of the lake is a must for visitors to Peru.

Jeepney

A jeepney is the most common form of public transportation in the Philippines. They are made out of the jeeps left on the islands by the American army at the end of World War II. People gave the jeeps a roof, put in two long seats on either side and painted them, turning them into small buses. Jeepneys have open windows instead of air conditioning. They're often packed with passengers and there are no bus stops – the driver just slows down to let the passengers jump on and off.

Dog sleds

Dog sledding is a unique experience because it's something you can't do in many other parts of the world. It was once the only way to get around in the snow of Alaska, but now its use is limited to winter sports and tourism. The best time to try it is from January to March – in the summer there isn't enough snow, so the dogs pull sleds on wheels. The ride can be a little bumpy because the sled sometimes goes over stones and the dogs bark a lot. All the same, it's an opportunity not to be missed.

b Read the article again. Mark the sentences T (true) or F (false).

1. Noris are a good way to see Cambodian cities. _F_
2. The train fare is not always the same. ___
3. Totora reed boats are made from special plants. ___
4. Today the boats are only used to carry tourists. ___
5. Jeepneys are used by the military to transport soldiers. ___
6. There are usually a lot of people in jeepneys. ___
7. Most people in Alaska don't travel by dog sled anymore. ___
8. Dog sleds are a very relaxing way to travel. ___

c Look at the highlighted words and phrases. What do you think they mean? Use your dictionary to look up their meaning and pronunciation.

6 LISTENING

a **ONLINE** Listen to the experiences of five speakers who were doing dangerous things while they were driving. Match the speakers with the things they were doing.

Speaker 1 _E_ A Putting on makeup
Speaker 2 __   B Listening to his/her favorite music
Speaker 3 __   C Writing a text message
Speaker 4 __   D Setting or adjusting a GPS
Speaker 5 __   E Talking on a cell phone

b Listen again and answer the questions.

1. What did Speaker 1's car crash into? _A van_
2. How far had Speaker 2 driven past Denver before she realized her mistake? _____
3. Where did Speaker 3 end up? _____
4. Who did Speaker 4 almost hit? _____
5. What color was the traffic light when the accident happened to Speaker 5? _____

c Listen again with the audioscript on p. 70.

USEFUL WORDS AND PHRASES

Learn these words and phrases.

adjust (GPS) /əˈdʒʌst/
reach /ritʃ/
be ahead of /bi əˈhɛd əv/
crash (into) /kræʃ/
get stuck (in a traffic jam) /gɛt ˈstʌk/
get worse /gɛt ˈwərs/
turn red /tərn ˈrɛd/
turn around /tərn əˈraʊnd/
do your hair /du yər hɛr/
put on makeup /pʊt ɑn ˈmeɪkʌp/

Men want to be a woman's first love. Women like to be a man's last romance.

Oscar Wilde, Irish writer

3B Stereotypes – or are they?

1 GRAMMAR articles: *a / an*, *the*, no article

a Circle the correct answers.

1 I think *girls* / *the girls* are better at learning *languages* / *the languages* than *boys* / *the boys*.
2 Did you lock *door* / *the door* when you left *house* / *the house* this morning?
3 My sister works for *Japanese* / *a Japanese* company. She's *engineer* / *an engineer*.
4 I don't usually like *fish* / *the fish*, but *salmon* / *the salmon* we had last night was delicious.
5 We go to *movies* / *the movies* once *a week* / *the week*.
6 Don't worry! It's not *the end* / *end* of *the world* / *world*.
7 Do you think *women* / *the women* are more sensitive than *men* / *the men*?
8 What *beautiful* / *a beautiful* day! Let's have *lunch* / *a lunch* on the patio.

b Are the highlighted phrases right (✓) or wrong (✗)? Correct the wrong phrases.

1 That's pretty dress – the color suits you. ✗
    a pretty dress
2 He's hoping to visit his parents the next weekend. ☐
    _____
3 The money doesn't make people happy. ☐
    _____
4 My grandfather left school when he was 14. ☐
    _____
5 They go to the dentist about twice the year. ☐
    _____
6 Have you watched DVD that I lent you? ☐
    _____
7 That was one of the best meals I've ever had. ☐
    _____
8 What noisy child! Where are his parents? ☐
    _____
9 Alex is studying to become doctor. ☐
    _____
10 I love the cats, but my boyfriend doesn't like them. ☐
    _____
11 Her husband sits in front of the TV all day. ☐
    _____
12 She always gets to the work at five-thirty. ☐
    _____

2 PRONUNCIATION /ə/, sentence stress, /ðə/ or /ði/?

a ONLINE Listen and complete the sentences.

1 I'd like to __speak__ to the __manager__.
2 I put the _____ on the _____.
3 _____ are we going to _____ tonight?
4 Could you _____ the _____ for a minute?
5 She needs to see a _____ about her _____.
6 We want to _____ for a _____ tomorrow.

b Listen again and repeat. Copy the rhythm.

c ONLINE Listen and repeat the phrases. Pay attention to the pronunciation of *the*.

1 The conversation was about the woman next door.
2 The university invited a guest to speak at the meeting.
3 I sometimes go to the theater in the evening.
4 We took the elevator instead of walking up the stairs.
5 The office gave me all the information I needed.
6 The gray skirt is nice, but I prefer the black one.

3 READING

a Read the article once and put the headings in the correct place.

A Men are better navigators than women
B Women talk more than men
C Men don't see colors as well as women

Stereotypes supported by science

1 _____

Men have a reputation for wearing clothes that don't look good together – if men do look good, it's because their girlfriends or wives have helped them get dressed. Why's that?

Science says: Let's take a look at chromosomes – the parts of our DNA that control many things about us. The color red is carried only by the X chromosome. Women have two X chromosomes, and so they are more likely to be able to see red. Men only have one X chromosome. How we see color depends on the ability to see red, blue, and green, so women are more likely to see colors better. Being able to see colors well was important in prehistoric times when women looked for fruit for food. They had to be able to tell the difference between the types of fruit on the trees so that they didn't choose a type that was poisonous. For them, seeing different colors meant they could survive.

2 _____

Most men have a natural ability to read maps while women usually need to turn them around. How come?

Science says: Men are able to see the size and position of things much quicker than women. This ability is called "spatial awareness". Researchers discovered in a study of four-year-old children that only one girl has this ability for every four boys. Once again, the explanation can be found in the past. Do you remember those prehistoric women? Well, while they were looking for fruit, the men traveled long distances to hunt animals. When they had caught enough, they had to find their way home again. And this is where they learned "spatial awareness." The women didn't need it because they hardly ever went out of sight of their homes, but for the men, it was vital.

3 _____

Humans are social animals, so why is it that men don't like sharing their problems while women tell their best friends everything?

Science says: The answer is in the brain. The parts responsible for language are 17% larger in a woman's brain than in a man's brain. Also, women use both the left and the right side of the brain to use language, while men use only one side – their strongest side. And there's more. The part of the brain that connects the two parts together – the corpus callosum – is larger in women too, which means that they can move information from one part to the other part more quickly. Nobody is sure why these differences exist, but it's clear that women have a definite advantage over men when it comes to communication.

b Read the article again. Choose the right answers.

1 Men can find it difficult to perceive…
  a three colors.
  (b) one color.
  c any colors.
2 Seeing colors well helped prehistoric women…
  a find interesting things to eat.
  b cook food correctly.
  c choose the right fruit.
3 The results of the study showed that…
  a four-year-olds don't have spatial awareness.
  b boys learn spatial awareness before girls.
  c girls don't have spatial awareness.
4 Women didn't need spatial awareness in prehistoric times because…
  a the men were always with them.
  b they never left home.
  c they didn't travel far from home.
5 Men are worse at communicating because…
  a part of their brains is smaller.
  b their brains are 17% smaller.
  c their brains are larger.
6 The function of the corpus callosum in the brain is…
  a to communicate between both sides.
  b to store different languages.
  c to control the language process.

c Look at the highlighted words and phrases. What do you think they mean? Use your dictionary to look up their meaning and pronunciation.

d Complete the sentences with one of the highlighted words or phrases.

1 It's a _definite_ _advantage_ to have good test scores if you want to go to college.
2 Don't eat those mushrooms you found outside! They could be _____.
3 Who's _____ _____ making this mess?
4 She's _____ _____ to accept if you invite her husband as well.
5 Italian people _____ _____ _____ for being great cooks.
6 It's _____ that I finish the report before the end of the day.

4 VOCABULARY collocation: verbs / adjectives + prepositions

a Circle the correct prepositions.

1 They're arriving *at | on | in* Seoul on Friday.
2 That suitcase belongs *for | from | to* me.
3 We should ask someone *at | for | of* directions.
4 We might go camping, but it depends *in | of | on* the weather.
5 Everybody laughed *about | at | to* me when I fell off the chair.
6 Who's going to pay *for | of | with* the meal?
7 I dreamed *about | from | with* my old school friends last night.
8 That girl reminds me *about | of | to* my cousin.

b Complete the sentences with the correct prepositions.

1 Tony used to be married __to__ Teresa.
2 You can rely _____ me to help you with the party tomorrow.
3 They're worried _____ their teenage son.
4 We're not very interested _____ abstract art.
5 I'm very different _____ my sister.
6 Adam's very good _____ math.
7 I'm fed up _____ this weather.
8 He's famous _____ his role in *Sherlock Holmes*.

5 WHEN ARE PREPOSITIONS STRESSED?

a ONLINE Listen and complete the dialogues.

1 A Who did you __argue__ __with__?
  B I _____ with my _____.
2 A Who are you _____ _____?
  B I'm _____ at _____!
3 A What are you so _____ _____?
  B I'm _____ about my _____.
4 A What are you _____ _____?
  B I'm _____ to the _____.

b Listen again and repeat. Copy the rhythm.

6 LISTENING

a ONLINE Listen to a radio call-in program. Which speaker has the most traditional view about men doing the cooking?

1 Nick ☐   2 Eve ☐   3 Frank ☐   4 Martina ☐

b Listen again and mark the sentences T (true) or F (false).

1 Nick is unemployed. __T__
2 He wouldn't like to be a chef. __
3 Eve cooks all the meals at her house. __
4 She spends a lot of time cleaning the kitchen. __
5 Frank thinks that girls work harder than they used to. __
6 Frank thinks that girls nowadays can cook. __
7 Martina's partner does all the cooking. __
8 Martina respects men who can cook. __T__

c Listen again with the audioscript on p. 71.

USEFUL WORDS AND PHRASES

Learn these words and phrases.

claim (vb) /kleɪm/
reduce /rɪˈdus/
almost /ˈɔlmoʊst/
slightly /ˈslaɪtli/
whereas /wɛrˈæz/
according to /əˈkɔrdɪŋ tu/
in fact /ɪn ˈfækt/
range from /ˈreɪndʒ frəm/
tend to /ˈtɛnd tə/
be skeptical of /bi ˈskɛptɪkl əv/

ONLINE FILE 3

Practical English A difficult celebrity

1 GIVING OPINIONS

Complete the dialogue.

John I love this song. Can you turn it up?
Anna Do I have to? It's really old.
John It may be old, but it's one of my favorites. ¹P_ersonally_, I think pop music was better in the past than it is now. What do you ² th_____?
Anna No, I don't think that's ³ r_____. In my ⁴ op_____, there is some great music around. And some of today's singers have amazing voices.
John I ⁵ ag_____. But very few of them write their own music. If you ⁶ as_____ me, the real musicians are the ones who write the songs and then perform them live on stage. Don't you ⁷ ag_____?
Anna To be ⁸ h_____, I don't know a lot about it. I just turn the radio on and listen to what they're playing!

2 SOCIAL ENGLISH

Complete the dialogues. Use a phrase containing the word in parentheses.

1 **A** Hello! _I'm back_! (back)
   B Hi! Did you have a good day?
2 **A** I'm going out for a walk now. Do you want to come?
   B _____ _____. I'll get my coat. (minute)
3 **A** I brought you some flowers.
   B Thank you. That's _____ _____. (kind)
4 **A** _____ _____ what you said about moving to California? (mean)
   B Yes. I think it'll be a great opportunity for us.
5 **A** You look upset. What's the matter.
   B Nothing really. _____ _____ my boyfriend's away and I really miss him. (just)

3 READING

a Read the text. Mark the sentences T (true) or F (false).

1 New York taxis are all the same model of car. _F_
2 A medallion number has four numbers and one letter. ___
3 An off-duty cab won't pick you up. ___
4 You should stand in the street until a taxi stops for you. ___
5 When you get in a taxi, the price starts at 50 cents. ___
6 You pay per minute if you are not moving. ___
7 Taxi drivers like to be paid in cash. ___

NEW YORK TAXIS

New York taxis provide an essential service to New Yorkers and tourists for getting around the city. There are over 12,000 yellow medallion taxicabs so it doesn't take long to see one.

What does a New York taxi look like?
New York taxis come in many different shapes and sizes, but to be official taxis they must be yellow. They must also have a special code called a medallion number: one number, then one letter, and two more numbers. A bronze badge with the same code should also be displayed on the hood.
Only taxis with the above are legally licensed to pick you up!

How will I know when a New York taxi is available?
It's all in the lights! When just the center light illuminates the medallion number, the taxi is available to be hailed. When the center light is off and both sidelights are on (illuminating the words "Off Duty"), the taxi is off duty. When no lights are illuminated, the taxi is already in use.

How to hail a New York taxi.
First, try to hail a taxi in the direction you are already going; it saves time and money. When you see an available taxi, make sure it's safe and step off the sidewalk while holding your hand up high. If for any reason you don't get the driver's attention, step back onto the sidewalk and wait for the next available taxi and repeat the process. It's as simple as that.

New York taxi fares.
Once you step into the cab the meter will be turned on. This is called the "flag-drop fare" and is $2.50. After that it will cost you 50 cents for every one-fifth of a mile, or 50 cents per minute if you are stuck in traffic. There is a flat-rate charge of $52 from Manhattan to JFK Airport.
If you're happy with the trip, you should tip your driver between 15% and 20% of the total fare. Paying by cash is preferred, however all taxis now accept credit cards.

b <u>Underline</u> five words or phrases you don't know. Use your dictionary to look up their meaning and pronunciation.

> Failure is not falling down. Failure is falling down and not getting up again.
> Richard Nixon, former US President

4A Failure and success

1 GRAMMAR can, could, be able to

a Circle the correct form. Check (✓) if both are correct.

1 She *can | is able to* swim really well because she used to live by the ocean. ✓
2 You don't need to *can | be able to* drive to live in the city.
3 Luke *could | was able to* read when he was only three years old.
4 If it doesn't rain tomorrow, *we can | we'll be able to* go for a long walk.
5 Sorry, I've been so busy that I *haven't could | haven't been able to* call until now.
6 If Maria had a less demanding job, she *could | would be able to* enjoy life more.
7 I've never *could | been able to* dance well, but I'd love to learn.
8 We're really sorry we *couldn't | weren't able to* come to your wedding.
9 I *used to can | used to be able to* speak a little Portuguese, but I've forgotten most of it now.
10 *Can you | Will you be able to* make it to dinner tonight?
11 To work for this company, you *must can | must be able to* speak at least three languages.
12 I hate *can't | not being able to* communicate with the local people when I'm traveling.

b Read Tyler Ruiz's résumé. Then complete the sentences with the correct form of *can*, *could*, or *be able to*.

1 Tyler ___can___ sail.
2 He _____ speak a little Chinese when he started working in Hong Kong.
3 He _____ speak German.
4 He _____ design websites since 1999.
5 He'd like _____ speak Russian.
6 He _____ finish his Ph.D. before he left the US.
7 He _____ speak a little Russian soon.

Name: Tyler Ruiz
Date of Birth: 09/22/1980

Education
Degree in French with Marketing (2003)
Master's in Business Administration (2006)
Started Ph.D. in Business (2009) – incomplete

Work Experience
1998–2000: Trainer and Operator with Texas Instruments, London
2003–2009: Assistant then Marketing Manager, Texas Instruments, Dallas, USA
2009–present: Managing Director, AHH Marketing Services Ltd., Hong Kong

Other Skills
IT skills – advanced.
Course in web design 1999.

Languages
French (fluent)   Chinese (basic) certificate 2008
I hope to start Russian classes next January.

Hobbies and Interests
Watersports, especially sailing and windsurfing

2 PRONUNCIATION sentence stress

ONLINE Listen and repeat the sentences. Copy the rhythm.

1 She can **sing very well**.
2 I've **never** been **able** to **ski**.
3 Can you **read** a **map**?
4 You **won't** be **able** to **go out tomorrow**.
5 He **hasn't** been **able** to **walk very fast** since he **hurt** his **leg**.
6 They **aren't able** to **come tonight**.

3 READING

a Read the article once and match paragraphs A–D with photos 1–4.

 Steven Spielberg 1
 Isaac Newton 2
 Bill Gates 3
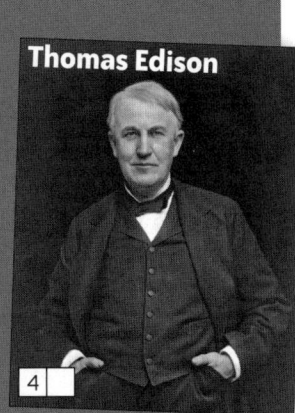 Thomas Edison 4

Failure: the first step toward success
Many people who have found success started out by failing.
Below are four of the most famous.

A Some people consider this man to be the greatest scientist who has ever lived. However, his early life was nothing special. He was very small as a child and he was a very bad student. When he was twelve, his mother took him out of school so that he could learn how to run the family farm. Unfortunately, he wasn't very good at that either, so in the end he was sent back to school. After *eventually* passing his exams, he went to Cambridge University where he became a brilliant scholar. Later, he developed his law of gravity.

B This man is one of the most famous inventors of all time, which is incredible when you think he only went to school for three months. After his teacher *lost patience* with him, his mother taught him at home and he learned many important lessons from reading books. His working life started as badly as his schooling had, and he *was fired* from his first two jobs. However, this gave him more time to experiment – by the end of his life he had invented over a thousand devices. His most famous invention was a certain type of lightbulb.

C Ask anyone to name the most famous movie director in Hollywood and many of them will say this man's name. However, his movie career started badly, as he was rejected three times from film school. He eventually started his studies at a different school, but he *dropped out* to become a director before he had finished. Since then he has won the Oscar for best director twice, and three of his movies have broken *box office* records. He went back to school in 2002 to finish his studies and earn his BA degree.

D Although he is one of the most successful businessmen and computer programmers of all time, this man didn't actually finish college. He was very bright at school and went to Harvard University, but he spent most of his time using the college's computers for his own projects and didn't do much studying. After dropping out, he decided to start his own company with a friend. This company failed, but he persisted and won a contract with IBM which eventually resulted in his company becoming one of the most powerful and recognized *brands* in the world today.

b Read the article again. Mark the sentences T (true) or F (false).

1 Isaac Newton almost became a farmer. *T*
2 He was never a very good student. ___
3 Thomas Edison missed three months of school when he was a child. ___
4 He didn't make a good impression on his bosses at the start of his working life. ___
5 Steven Spielberg couldn't go to the film school he wanted to. ___
6 He has never finished his degree. ___
7 Bill Gates failed out of college. ___
8 His first company wasn't successful. ___

c Look at the *highlighted* words and phrases. What do you think they mean? Use your dictionary to look up their meaning and pronunciation.

d Complete the sentences with one of the *highlighted* words or phrases.

1 The child's parents *lost patience* with her and sent her to her room.
2 He wasn't enjoying college, so he _____ _____ after the first year.
3 After several months, she _____ managed to persuade her boyfriend to see an opera.
4 My colleague _____ _____ for sending personal emails from work.
5 My husband refuses to buy expensive _____ of clothing.
6 There was a huge line at the _____ _____ because it was the opening night of the movie.

4 VOCABULARY -ed / -ing adjectives

a Right (✓) or wrong (✗)? Correct the wrong adjectives.

1 Turn the channel! This is a bored TV show. ✗
   _____boring_____
2 Taking care of small children can be very tired. ☐
   _____
3 His test scores were very disappointing. ☐
   _____
4 I was very embarrassed when my phone rang in the meeting. ☐
   _____
5 Junko was very surprising because she didn't know they were coming. ☐
   _____
6 We took a lot of pictures because the view was so amazing. ☐
   _____
7 Are you interested in car racing? ☐
   _____
8 She felt frustrating because she couldn't get on the surfboard. ☐
   _____

b Complete the sentences with the correct form of the adjectives in parentheses.

1 I enjoyed the book, but the movie was a little __boring__. (bored / boring)
2 I felt very _____ when I realized my mistake. (embarrassed / embarrassing)
3 He's _____ because the printer isn't working. (frustrated / frustrating)
4 The final quarter of the game was really _____. (excited / exciting)
5 We haven't heard from her since she arrived in Bangkok – it's very _____. (worried / worrying)
6 Your trip sounds really _____ – tell me more! (interested / interesting)
7 I'm tired of this terrible weather – it's so _____. (depressed / depressing)
8 Max was very _____ when he wasn't chosen for the job. (disappointed / disappointing)

c Circle the -ed adjectives in exercise b where -ed is pronounced /ɪd/.

Reflexive pronouns

d Complete the sentences with the correct word.

1 The best way to get healthy is to make __yourself__ exercise every day.
2 Jon and Danny help _____ to food whenever they come to my house.
3 Jenna painted the bathroom _____.
4 The computer turns _____ off if nobody uses it for a while.
5 I always sing to _____ when I'm in the shower.
6 We found the apartment _____, without any help from a real estate agent.

5 LISTENING

a **ONLINE** You are going to hear five speakers talking about mistakes they have made in a foreign language. Listen and complete the sentences.

Speaker 1 was speaking __French__ to _____.
Speaker 2 was speaking _____ to _____.
Speaker 3 was speaking _____ to _____.
Speaker 4 was speaking _____ to _____.
Speaker 5 was speaking _____ to _____.

b Listen again and complete the table.

	What they wanted to say	What they actually said
Speaker 1	inhaler	
Speaker 2		
Speaker 3		
Speaker 4		
Speaker 5		

c Listen again with the audioscript on p. 71.

USEFUL WORDS AND PHRASES

Learn these words and phrases.

link /lɪŋk/
scuba dive /ˈskubə daɪv/
skills /skɪlz/
(dance) steps /stɛps/
multilingual /mʌltiˈlɪŋgwəl/
fluently /ˈfluəntli/
basic phrases /beɪsɪk ˈfreɪzɪz/
language barrier /ˈlæŋgwɪdʒ bæriər/
teach yourself books /ˈtitʃ yərˈsɛlf bʊks/
more exceptions than rules /mɔr ɪkˈsɛpʃnz ðən rulz/

> When a man opens the car door for his wife it's either a new car or a new wife.
> *Duke of Edinburgh, husband of Queen Elizabeth II*

4B Modern manners?

1 VOCABULARY phone language

Complete the sentences.

1 You must not use your phone in a qu<u>iet</u> z<u>one</u>.
2 When you finish a phone call, you h_____ u_____.
3 If someone doesn't answer their phone, you can leave a m_____ on their v_____.
4 If you're in a meeting, you can put your phone on s_____ or v_____ mode.
5 If someone's phone is off, you can c_____ b_____ later.
6 The sound your cell phone makes when someone calls you is a r_____.
7 If you want to text your friends more cheaply, you can use in_____ m_____.
8 When you call someone, you have to d_____ their number by pressing some keys.
9 If someone is already talking on their cell phone when you call, the line is b_____.
10 You can protect the display of your cell phone or computer with a sc_____.

2 GRAMMAR modals of obligation: *must, have to, should*

a Circle the correct form. Check (✓) if both are possible.

b Correct any mistakes in use or form in the highlighted phrases. Check (✓) the correct sentences.

1 People must not use their cell phones when they're talking to you.
   People shouldn't use
2 I must go to work by bus yesterday. My car was being repaired.
   _____
3 Do you have to wear a suit and tie at work?
   _____
4 You don't have to play soccer here. It says "no ball games."
   _____
5 My father is a taxi driver and he should work nights.
   _____
6 I didn't have to cook last night because we went out for dinner.
   _____
7 In the future, maybe everyone must speak English and Chinese.
   _____
8 You don't look well. You should to go home.
   _____

What you need to know before you visit the US

1 You *have to / must* have a visa to enter the country. ✓
2 You *must not / don't have to* drive on the left! Here we drive on the right!
3 You *must not / don't have to* pay to visit most museums and art galleries. Entrance is usually free.
4 You *have to / should* go on a ferry to visit the Statue of Liberty. You can't go by bus.
5 You *have to / must* wear a seat belt at all times in a car.
6 You *must / should* always try to arrive on time for an appointment or meeting. Americans are very punctual!
7 If you are sightseeing in New York, you *must / should* buy a MetroCard that gives you cheaper travel on the subway and buses.
8 You *must not / don't have to* smoke in any public building. It is prohibited by law.
9 When talking to Americans, you *shouldn't / don't have to* ask them about their salary. Some people might think this is rude.
10 You *must / have to* answer some questions when you go through immigration.

3 PRONUNCIATION silent consonants, linking

a Cross out the silent consonant in the words.
1 write
2 receipt
3 hour
4 shouldn't
5 exhausted
6 walk
7 could
8 debt

b ONLINE Listen and check. Then listen again and repeat the words.

c Listen and repeat the sentences. Try to link the words.
1 You shouldn't talk on the phone when you're driving.
2 You must always wear your seat belt in the car.
3 You don't have to wear a uniform.
4 You shouldn't ask a friend for money.
5 You have to watch out for pickpocketers.
6 You should take a present for them.

d ONLINE Listen and check. Then listen again and repeat the sentences.

4 READING

a Read the article once and check (✓) the best summary.
1 How men should behave toward women in the 21st century. ☐
2 How men behaved toward women in the past. ☐
3 The difference between men's and women's manners. ☐

Ladies first?

Nobody knows how long people have been using the words "Ladies First," nor is anyone sure where the concept came from. However, neither of these facts matters today. The important question is whether the tradition is still relevant, and if men should continue respecting it.

In the past, there was a strict set of rules concerning men's behavior toward women – or rather "ladies" as they were called then. Men wearing hats used to take them off in the presence of women. They used to stand up whenever a woman entered or left a room, and they did the same at a dining table. Men used to hold a door for a woman to allow her to go through first. They always used to pay for meals – but we'll come back to that one later. All of these customs were considered good manners, and people looked down on men who did not conform.

In fact, this set of rules actually made things easier for men. If they broke a rule, they knew perfectly well that they were going to offend somebody. Today, it is much easier to cause offense without meaning to. For example, if a man opens a door to let a woman through first, and she does so without saying thank you, the man may feel offended. And if a man invites a woman to a restaurant of his choice on their first date, and then asks her to pay her half of the check, it may be the woman who gets upset. Women no longer want to be treated as the weaker sex, which leaves men in a dilemma. On one hand, men are conscious of the "Ladies First" tradition, but on the other, they do not want to offend. Often, they don't know what to do.

The best advice is this: if in doubt, men should follow the rules of "Ladies First." Even if the woman considers the behavior inappropriate, she will still realize that the man has good manners. This is particularly relevant on that first date we were talking about. If the man has invited the woman out, then he should pay the check. Actually, it's the invitation to dinner itself that is important here, not the amount of money spent. In general, women appreciate a picnic or a home-made dinner just as much as an expensive meal.

So the answer to our original question is: yes. "Ladies First" is still relevant today, but not in the same way as it was in the past. Most women appreciate a kind gesture made by a man, but he should never accompany it with the words "Ladies First" – it spoils the effect completely!

b Read the article again and choose the right answer.
1 According to the article…
    a the idea of "Ladies first" started in the Middle Ages.
    b the idea of "Ladies first" is a new idea.
    c it's not known when the idea of "Ladies first" started.
2 In the past…
    a men didn't know how to behave toward women.
    b "Ladies first" was very polite.
    c it didn't matter if men broke the rules.
3 Nowadays, men…
    a aren't sure how to behave toward women.
    b behave in the same way toward women.
    c have new rules to follow.
4 According to the article, men should…
    a not think about what women want.
    b follow the rules of "Ladies first."
    c not follow the rules of "Ladies first."
5 According to the article, women…
    a always want expensive things.
    b don't like it when men cook.
    c like a meal at home or in a restaurant.

c Look at the highlighted words and phrases. What do you think they mean? Use your dictionary to look up their meaning and pronunciation.

d Find the highlighted words or phrases in the text to match the definitions.
1 not right for a particular situation
   inappropriate
2 an action that shows other people how you feel
   _____
3 understand the value of something
   _____
4 an idea
   _____
5 upset somebody
   _____
6 thought they were better than
   _____

5 LISTENING

a **ONLINE** Listen to a radio program about good manners in different countries. What kind of advice do the four people ask about? Check (✓) the correct answers. There is one piece of advice you do not need to use.
1 Advice about how to behave in business situations. ☐
2 Advice about body language. ☐
3 Advice about meeting new people. ✓
4 Advice about forming a line. ☐
5 Advice about visiting someone's house. ☐

b Listen again and choose the right answers.
1 According to the expert, in Thailand you should not give a "wai" to…
    a people who are older than you.
    b anyone.
    c people who are younger than you.
2 When is it polite to say thank you in Brazil?
    a when a friend offers you a drink
    b when a stranger opens a door
    c both a and b are correct
3 Which gesture, often made by police officers, is an insult in Greece?
    a "Come here."
    b "Stop."
    c "Go away."
4 A foreign person in Korea…
    a must not bow to anyone.
    b must bow to everyone.
    c can bow to show politeness.
5 According to the expert, if a Korean person is happy, they bow very…
    a quickly.
    b slowly.
    c deeply.

c Listen again with the audioscript on p. 71.

USEFUL WORDS AND PHRASES

Learn these words and phrases.

etiquette /ˈɛtəkət/
manners /ˈmænərz/
host / hostess /hoʊst/ /ˈhoʊstəs/
behave /bɪˈheɪv/
deserve /dɪˈzɜrv/
disturb /dɪˈstɜrb/
inappropriate /ɪnəˈproʊpriət/
insulting /ɪnˈsʌltɪŋ/
allergic to /əˈlɜrdʒɪk tə/
should have (written) /ʃʊd əv/

ONLINE **FILE 4**

> It's not whether you win or lose that matters, but whether I win or lose.
> Sandy Lyle, Scottish golfer

5A Sports superstitions

1 GRAMMAR past tenses

Complete the sentences with the correct form of the verbs in parentheses. Use the simple past, past continuous, or past perfect.

1 We were late. When we _arrived_ (arrive), everyone else _had finished_ (finish) their lunch and they _were sitting_ (sit) on the patio having coffee.
2 They _____ (drive) to the airport when they suddenly _____ (remember) that they _____ (not turn off) the lights.
3 The game _____ (already / start) when we _____ (turn on) the TV. The Red Sox _____ (lose) and they _____ (play) very badly.
4 I _____ (not recognize) many people at my old school reunion because everyone _____ (change) a lot in twenty years.
5 My sister _____ (wait) to go out for dinner yesterday when her boyfriend _____ (call) her to say that he _____ (not can) come because his car _____ (break down).
6 Real Madrid _____ (beat) Barcelona yesterday. Barcelona _____ (win) 1–0 in the first half, but Madrid _____ (score) two goals in the second half.
7 He _____ (run) to the station, but the nine o'clock train _____ (already / leave). The station was empty except for two people who _____ (wait) for the next train.
8 It _____ (start) raining when I _____ (walk) to work. I _____ (call) a car service because I _____ (not wear) a coat and I _____ (not have) an umbrella.

2 PRONUNCIATION /ɔr/, /ər/

a Circle the word with a different sound.

1 horse	2 bird	3 horse	4 bird
four	first	course	court
shorts	hurt	floor	serve
w**ar**m up	sports	score	shirt
(work out)	world	worst	worse

b **ONLINE** Listen and check. Then listen again and repeat the words.

3 READING

a Read the article on p. 31 once. Complete the sentences.

 1 The boy was playing _____.
 2 He cheated by taking _____.

b Read the article again. Mark the sentences T (true) or F (false).

 1 According to the article, people usually learn not to cheat when they are young children. _F_
 2 Blank tiles can be used when players don't have the right letter. __
 3 The boy was one of the best players in the tournament. __
 4 The previous day, the boy had beaten Arthur Moore. __
 5 Moore caught the boy while he was making a word. __
 6 He saw the boy take a blank tile out of his pocket. __
 7 The boy answered the tournament director's questions truthfully. __
 8 He wasn't allowed to continue playing. __

c Look at the highlighted words and phrases. What do you think they mean? Use your dictionary to look up their meaning and pronunciation.

d Complete the sentences with one of the highlighted words or phrases.

 1 James _discretely_ bought the present when his wife wasn't looking.
 2 Sam _____ telling lies about her colleagues.
 3 The athlete was _____ after he made three false starts.
 4 My computer is broken, so I'm going to _____ it with a new one.
 5 She became _____ when she found the train tickets in his pocket.
 6 He couldn't _____ the man of lying because there was no proof he had done anything bad.
 7 Jack beat his _____ 6–1, 6–3.
 8 They _____ to stealing after they lost their jobs.

30

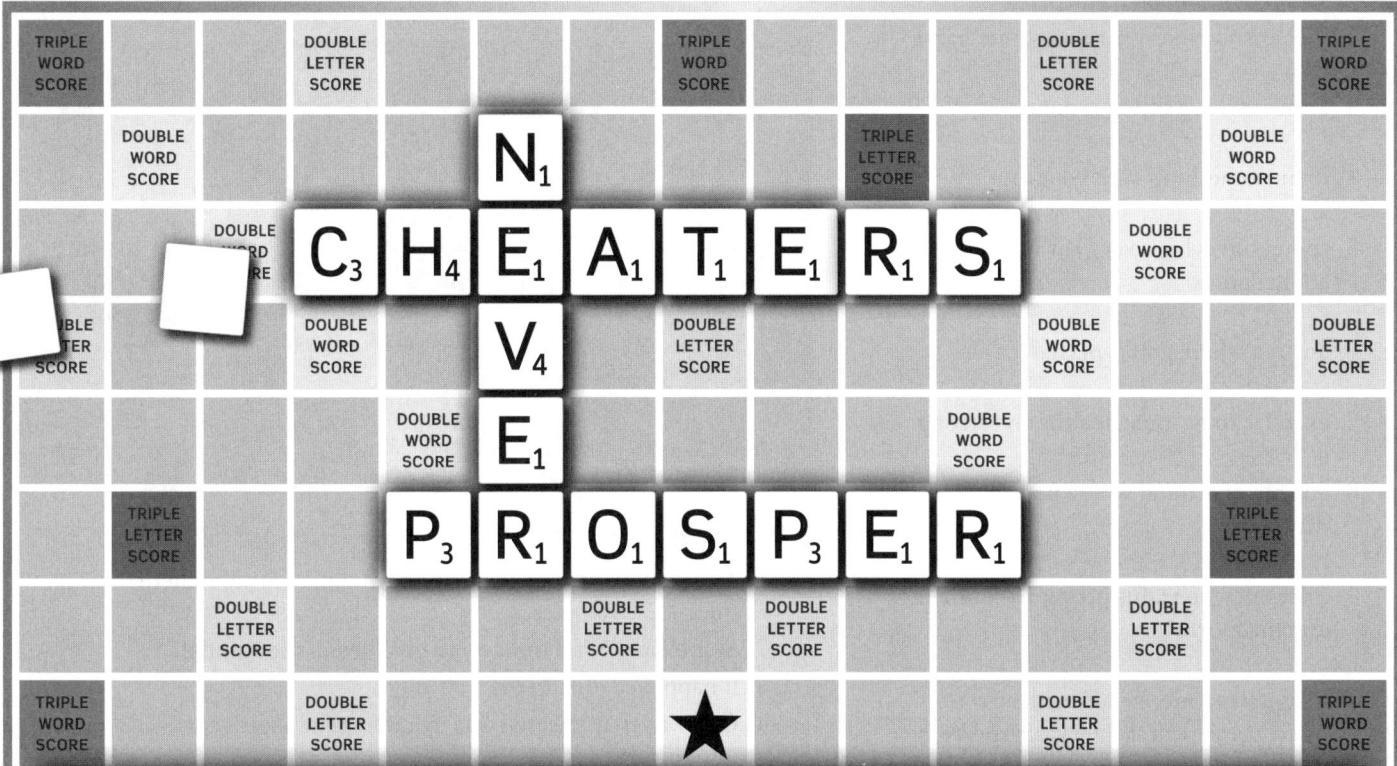

It's normal for young children to cheat when they're playing board games. As they grow older, they realize that the fun is actually in taking part in the game, not necessarily in winning it. By the time they reach their teens, they have usually learned not to cheat. Sadly, this was not the case for a player in a national board game championship held annually in the US. The player wanted to win so much that he resorted to cheating.

The board game was Scrabble. This is a word game that was created in 1938 by an American architect named Alfred Mosher Butts. In the game, players have to make words from individual letters on small squares called "tiles," and then put the words on a board. Two of the most useful tiles in the game are the blanks, which are tiles without any letters on them. A blank isn't worth any points, but a player can use it to replace any letter of the alphabet.

The cheater in this particular tournament was a 15-year-old boy from Orlando, Florida. He had surprised organizers in the early stages of the competition by beating some of the best players, despite the fact that he had never played in competitions before. This made some of the other players suspicious, including the man who caught him, 43-year-old Arthur Moore. Moore had already played the boy the day before, and Moore had won the game, although the boy had had both of the blank tiles. In Scrabble, before a new game starts, the players put the tiles from the previous game back into a small bag. This time, Moore had a good look at the tiles on the table before he and his opponent put them in the bag to start the game. He was not surprised to see that the two blanks were together on the table in front of the boy. As the two players were putting the tiles into the bag, Moore discretely watched the boy's left hand. He saw the boy pick up the two blanks, and put his hand under the table. This was the signal for Moore to call one of the organizers and accuse the boy of cheating.

When the boy was taken away for questioning, he admitted to taking the two blanks during the game and hiding them under the table. As a result of his cheating, the tournament director disqualified him and banned him from playing in the competition again.

4 VOCABULARY sports

a Read the definitions and write the words.
1 an area of water that swimmers use
   sw*imming* p*ool*
2 the person who controls a soccer game
   r_____
3 an area where skiing is done
   s_____
4 to hit something with your foot
   k_____
5 somebody who is very enthusiastic about sports
   f_____
6 an area where golf is played
   c_____
7 exercise to become healthy and strong
   g_____ in s_____
8 an area of ground where people play soccer
   f_____
9 a person who trains people to compete in certain sports
   c_____
10 a large structure, usually with no roof, where people can sit and watch sports
   st_____

b Complete the sentences with the simple past of the verbs in the box.

| beat   get injured   lose   play   score |
| throw   tie   train   warm up   win |

1 The US *played* Russia last night for the championship.
2 The team _____ hard every day before the tournament.
3 The Canadian runner _____ the race. He got the gold medal.
4 The players _____ _____ by jogging and doing easy exercises just before the game started.
5 Joe _____ the score when he hit a home run!
6 I didn't play well in the semifinal round. I _____ 2–6, 1–6.
7 Marc _____ the ball to his brother, but his brother dropped it.
8 Brazil _____ Sweden. They had a much better team.
9 The Argentinian striker _____ four goals in the last game.
10 Our best player _____ _____ in the second half, and was taken off the field to see the team's doctor.

5 LISTENING

a **ONLINE** Listen to a radio program about a sports scandal. Which country won the competition in the end?
_____

b Listen again and mark the sentences T (true) or F (false).
1 The scandal happened during the tennis tournament of the 2012 Olympics. _F_
2 South Korea and India were involved in the scandal. ___
3 It happened during the first stage. ___
4 One way they cheated was by hitting the shuttlecock into the net. ___
5 The same thing happened in another match. ___
6 The teams cheated because they had been offered money. ___
7 The crowd didn't enjoy the matches. ___
8 South Korea won the silver medal. ___

c Listen again with the audioscript on p. 72.

USEFUL WORDS AND PHRASES

Learn these words and phrases.

fate /feɪt/
rituals /ˈrɪtʃuəlz/
superstition /supərˈstɪʃn/
bounce /baʊns/
cheat /tʃit/
reveal /rɪˈvil/
sweat /swɛt/
a lucky charm /ə ˈlʌki tʃɑrm/
result in /rɪˈzʌlt ɪn/
tie your shoelaces /taɪ yər ˈʃuleɪsɪz/

Love is like war: easy to begin but very hard to stop.
HL Mencken, US journalist

5B Love at Exit 19

1 GRAMMAR usually and used to

a Correct any mistakes in the highlighted phrases. Check (✓) the correct sentences.

1 Where did you used to live before you moved here?
   did you use to live?
2 Jerry used to have a beard, but he shaved it off last week.
   ✓
3 I usually go to the gym when I leave work.
   _____
4 My wife doesn't use to wear makeup. She doesn't like it.
   _____
5 Did you use to have long hair?
   _____
6 I use to walk to work. My office is only ten minutes from my house.
   _____
7 Carol didn't used to talk to me, but now she always says hello.
   _____
8 Do you use to get up late on Sundays?
   _____
9 Did you used to watch cartoons when you were little?
   _____
10 We don't usually stay in expensive hotels, but this weekend is special.
   _____

b Complete the sentences with *usually* or the correct form of *used to*, and the verbs in parentheses.

1 She __used to wear__ glasses, but now she has contact lenses. (wear)
2 He _____ animals, but now he has a dog. (not like)
3 I _____ my parents on Sunday. It's good to talk to them. (call)
4 I _____ French classes, but I stopped because I don't have time now. (take)
5 We never _____, but now we go to restaurants twice a week. (eat out)
6 I _____ late, but today I have a lot to do. (not work)
7 My sister _____ very shy, but now she's confident. (be)
8 They _____ me a present on my birthday, but this year they forgot! (give)

2 PRONUNCIATION sentence stress; the letter s

a **ONLINE** Listen and repeat. Copy the rhythm.

1 **Where** did you **use** to **live**?
2 Did you **use** to **wear glasses**?
3 They **used** to **have** a lot of **money**.
4 He **used** to **go** to my **school**.
5 We **used** to **work together**.
6 You **used** to **have long hair**.
7 We **didn't use** to **get along**.
8 I **didn't use** to **like** it.

b Circle the word with a different sound.

1 snake	2 zebra	3 shower	4 television
see	eyes	tissue	usually
(friends)	easy	please	pleasure
most	especially	sure	decision
social	nowadays	sugar	music

c **ONLINE** Listen and check. Then listen again and repeat the words.

3 VOCABULARY relationships

a Complete the sentences with the people in the box.

classmates   close friend   colleague   couple
ex   fiancé   roommate   ~~wife~~

1 We're married.   She's my __wife__.
2 I share an apartment with her.   She's my _____.
3 I work with him.   He's my _____.
4 We used to go to school together.   We were _____.
5 I'm going to marry him.   He's my _____.
6 I used to go out with her.   She's my _____.
7 We've known each other for a long time. I tell her everything. She's a _____.
8 We've been going out together for three years. We're a _____.

b Complete the text with the simple past of the verbs in the box.

> be together   become friends   break up
> get along   get to know   get in touch   get married
> go out together   have (sth) in common
> lose touch   ~~meet~~   propose

Anna ¹ _met_ Luke when she started work. They ² _____ each other quickly because they sat next to each other in the office. They soon ³ _____ and they discovered that they ⁴ _____ a lot _____ because they were both sports fans. They ⁵ _____ a few times after work and they fell in love. They ⁶ _____ for a year, but they argued a lot, and in the end they ⁷ _____. After that, Anna got a new job in a different town and so they ⁸ _____. Ten years later, they ⁹ _____ again on Facebook. They were both still single and Mark had changed jobs, too. They decided to try again, and this time they ¹⁰ _____ better than before, maybe because they weren't working together. After six months, Luke ¹¹ _____ and Anna accepted. They ¹² _____ last spring. A lot of their old colleagues from work came to the wedding!

4 READING

a Read the article once. How many friends does the average American have?

_____.

Your friends in numbers

How many friends does the average person have? A researcher at Cornell University recently did a study to learn the number of friends a typical American has. He interviewed more than 2,000 adults aged 18 and over in his study. He asked them to list the names of the people they had discussed serious matters with in the last six months. About 48% of the people taking part gave the researcher one name, 18% gave him two, and about 29% gave him more than two.

These results contrast dramatically with the news published by the social networking site Facebook recently. They said that the average user on the site has 130 friends. The Cornell University study found the average number of friends to be a lot lower – 2.03 to be exact. The researcher from Cornell has explained that the difference lies in the definition of the word *friend*. A friend on Facebook may be a person who the user has met by chance or someone that they will never meet in real life. However, the friends in the researcher's study are close friends, who participants feel comfortable discussing their problems with.

In a similar study conducted 25 years ago, participants had a higher number of close friends. Then, the average number was three. Despite the lower number, the researcher does not believe that people are getting more isolated. Instead he thinks it's a sign that they are becoming better at choosing who they can trust with their secrets.

This is supported by the number of people in the study who could not think of any names of close friends they would discuss their personal problems with. The percentage of these participants is the same this time as it was 25 years ago. In both studies, just over 4% of the participants gave researchers no names. Apparently, the people who fall into this category are more likely to be men, or people with less education.

In general, the researcher from Cornell regards these findings as positive. In his opinion, they suggest that, at least in the case of Americans, people are not becoming less sociable.

b Read the article again and choose the best answer.

1 Most people in the Cornell University study had spoken about something important with…
   a one person.
   b two people.
   c more than two people.

2 The news published by Facebook is different from the results in the Cornell study because…
   a the people are different ages.
   b the studies are from different years.
   c the relationships aren't the same.

3 According to a previous study, people had _____ close friends in the past.
   a more
   b the same number of
   c fewer

4 The number of people with no close friends is _____ it was in the past.
   a higher than
   b the same as
   c lower than

5 The results of the Cornell study show that Americans today are _____ they used to be.
   a more sociable than
   b as sociable as
   c less sociable than

c Look at the highlighted words and phrases. What do you think they mean? Use your dictionary to look up their meaning and pronunciation.

d Complete the sentences with one of the highlighted words or phrases.

1 I found an old painting _by_ _chance_ while I was cleaning the attic.
2 I wouldn't _____ my son with my phone. He'd probably break it.
3 How much money does _____ _____ _____ earn per year?
4 They talked about _____ _____ first, and then moved on to the less important things.
5 The richer parts of town _____ _____ with the poorer outskirts.
6 Some teenagers are _____ _____ _____ because they spend so much time on their computers.

5 LISTENING

a ONLINE You are going to hear a radio program about research on love and attraction. Number the topics in the order you hear them.

   a How to use your eyes at a first meeting. ___
   b Body language at a first meeting. ___
   c How to use your voice at a first meeting. _1_
   d How much to smile at a first meeting. ___

b Listen again and mark the sentences T (true) or F (false).

1 It's very important to say the right thing the first time you talk to someone you like. _F_
2 A person's body language can make them more attractive. ___
3 Looking into someone's eyes can make them feel more attracted to you. ___
4 There were two weddings after an experiment in New York. ___
5 Standing up straight is a good way to keep someone's attention. ___
6 A person will copy your body language if they think you are interesting. ___
7 It is impossible to know if someone is smiling when you're talking to them on the phone. ___
8 Often when one person smiles, other people smile too. ___

c Listen again with the audioscript on p. 72.

USEFUL WORDS AND PHRASES

Learn these words and phrases.

candle /ˈkændl/
commuter /kəˈmyutər/
cute /kyut/
likely /ˈlaɪkli/
raise the barrier /reɪz ðə ˈbæriər/
addicted to (sth) /əˈdɪktəd tə/
night shifts /ˈnaɪt ʃɪfts/
turn out (to be) /tərn ˈaʊt/
exchange a few words /ɪksˈtʃeɪndʒ ə fyu wərdz/
find the courage (to do sth) /faɪnd ðə ˈkərɪdʒ/

ONLINE FILE 5

Practical English Old friends

1 PERMISSION AND REQUESTS

a Complete the requests with the correct form of the verbs in the box.

| ~~do~~ join pass meet take visit |

1 Could you _do_ me a big favor? [d]
2 Do you mind if I _____ you?
3 Would you mind _____ me at the airport?
4 Is it OK if we _____ my parents this weekend?
5 Can you _____ the salt?
6 Do you think you could _____ me to the train station?

b Match the requests from **a** with the responses a–f.

a Of course not. Take a seat.
b Sure. Here it is.
c Yes, of course. What time's your train?
d ~~It depends what it is!~~
e Not at all. When do you land?
f Sure. Which day would be best?

2 SOCIAL ENGLISH

Complete the dialogue.

Jay	Dan! It's great to ¹s_ee_ you.
Dan	You too, Jay. It's been years.
Jay	How ²c_____ you're so late?
Dan	My flight was delayed, and then I had to wait forever for a taxi.
Jay	Well, you're here now. Do you want something to eat?
Dan	No ³w_____, man! I want to go out and see the city!
Jay	Don't you want to unpack first?
Dan	No, I can do that later. But I'll take a shower, if you don't ⁴m_____.
Jay	Sure. Go ahead.
Dan	This is great. You and me getting ready to go out.
Jay	Yeah. It's just like the old ⁵d_____.
Dan	OK, I'm ready. Let's go. We have a lot to ⁶t_____ about.

3 READING Getting around the US

The US is huge, so flying is the quickest way to get around the country. It can be expensive though, so here are some other ways of getting around.

If you aren't in a hurry, the best alternative is to go by car. You have to be at least 25 years old to rent a car in the States, and you need a valid driver's license and a major credit card to do so. There are a lot of rental car companies, and their prices vary a lot. Compare companies before you decide which one to use, and remember it can be cheaper to book for a week than for a day.

If you prefer to be driven rather than driving yourself, the next best way to travel is by bus. Greyhound is the major long-distance bus company, and it has routes through the US and Canada. Tickets are much cheaper if you buy them seven days in advance, and there are often other offers. If you're traveling with a friend, your companion gets 50% off if you buy the tickets three days before you travel, and children between the ages of two and eleven get a 40% discount.

An alternative to using the bus is to take the train. Amtrak is the American rail company, and it has long-distance lines connecting all of the biggest cities. It also runs buses from major stations to smaller towns and national parks. Fares vary depending on the type of train and the seat, but you need to reserve at least three days ahead to get a discount. Students with an international student card get 15% off the regular fare. Bring your own food because the dining car is expensive.

a Read the text and answer the questions.

1 What do you need to rent a car in the US?
   You need a valid driver's license and a major credit card.
2 What is the difference between all the car rental companies?
3 Where does the Greyhound bus company operate?
4 How can you save money if you're traveling alone by bus?
5 How much do students pay on Amtrak trains?
6 What should long-distance rail passengers take with them?

b <u>Underline</u> five words or phrases you don't know. Use your dictionary to look up their meaning and pronunciation.

6A Shot on location

Film is one of three universal languages, the other two: mathematics and music.
Frank Capra, US movie director

1 VOCABULARY movies

a Read the clues. Complete the puzzle on the right to find the hidden kind of movie.

1. A movie where images are drawn is an an_imated_ movie.
2. A funny movie is a c_____.
3. A movie based on real events in the past is a h_____ movie.
4. A movie with an exciting plot is a th_____.
5. A scary movie is a h_____ movie.
6. A movie about cowboys is a w_____.
7. A movie with a serious story is a dr_____.
8. A funny movie about people falling in love is a r_____ comedy.
9. A movie about wars and battles is a w_____ m_____.
10. A movie where the cast sings and dances is a m_____.
11. A movie about imaginary events in the future is a sc_____-f_____ movie.

Hidden kind of movie: _____

THE MOVIE PUZZLE

b Complete the sentences.

1. The st_ar_ of the movie was a famous British actress.
2. I didn't understand the movie because the pl_____ was very complicated.
3. The actor accepted the part as soon as he read the sc_____.
4. Some members of the au_____ were crying at the end of the movie.
5. Most critics gave the movie an excellent r_____.
6. They only had to shoot the sc_____ once.
7. We don't speak French, so we saw the French movie with English s_____.
8. You'll have to wait for the s_____ to find out what happens next.
9. My favorite s_____ is the music from *The Artist*.
10. The best thing about the movie was the sp_____ ef_____. They looked very realistic.
11. The director is looking for ex_____ to appear in the crowd scenes.
12. The c_____ was a mixture of American and British actors.

2 GRAMMAR passive (all tenses)

a Complete the sentences with the correct passive form of the verbs in the box. Use the tense in parentheses.

direct dub invite play release shoot show write

1. The movie __is directed__ by Kathryn Bigelow. (simple present)
2. The part of Spider-Man _____ by Andrew Garfield. (simple past)
3. It was very windy while the scene _____. (past continuous)
4. The sequel _____ next year. (future, *will*)
5. Some of the extras _____ to the movie premiere. (future, *going to*)
6. The musical _____ in movie theaters all over the country. (present continuous)
7. The drama _____ into five other languages. (present perfect)
8. The script _____ by the author of the book. (simple past)

37

b **Circle** the correct form, active or passive.

Anna Karenina

Anna Karenina is a movie that ¹**directed** / **was directed** by Joe Wright. Most of the movie ²**shot** / **was shot** in an old theater outside of London, but some scenes ³**filmed** / **were filmed** in Russia. It ⁴**tells** / **is told** the story of a young Russian woman who is married to a government official, but ⁵**falls** / **is fallen** in love with an aristocrat. Keira Knightley ⁶**plays** / **is played** the part of Anna Karenina, and the part of her romantic interest, Count Vronsky, ⁷**plays** / **is played** by Aaron Taylor-Johnson.

The movie ⁸**starts** / **is started** when Anna arrives in Moscow. Her brother ⁹**has seen** / **has been seen** with another woman, and Anna must speak to her sister-in-law about the situation. It is during this meeting that Anna ¹⁰**introduces** / **is introduced** to the Count. The movie ¹¹**has based** / **is based** on the novel by Leo Tolstoy.

The superb soundtrack ¹²**composed** / **was composed** by Italian composer Dario Marianelli, who also ¹³**wrote** / **was written** the music for *Pride and Prejudice* and *Atonement*. Both of his previous soundtracks ¹⁴**nominated** / **were nominated** for Oscars, and *Atonement* won an Oscar.

3 PRONUNCIATION sentence stress

a **ONLINE** Listen and repeat the sentences. Copy the rhythm.

1 The **movie** is **based** on a **true story**.
2 These **scenes** will be **shot** on **location**.
3 The **actor** has been **nominated** for an **Oscar**.
4 The **script** was **written** by the **author** of the **novel**.
5 The **sequel** is **going** to be **released next week**.
6 The **costumes** are **being made** by **hand**.

b Underline the stressed syllable in these words.

1 au|di|ence
2 hi|stor|i|cal mo|vie
3 co|me|dy
4 di|rec|tor
5 dra|ma
6 hor|ror mo|vie
7 re|view
8 se|quel
9 sound|track
10 sub|ti|tles

c **ONLINE** Listen and check. Then listen again and repeat the words.

4 READING

a Read the text once. Check (✓) where you think it comes from.
1 an online newspaper ☐   3 a website for tourists ☐
2 a travel blog ☐   4 a movie program ☐

On location at Knebworth House

Knebworth House is famous worldwide for the major open-air rock concerts that have been held on its grounds since 1979. Knebworth is in the southeast England, and the Lytton family have lived there for over 500 years. The house itself is one of the oldest stately homes in the UK. It is also one of the most popular locations for the world's filmmakers.

Not surprisingly, the Gothic architecture of the house appealed to American movie director Tim Burton when he saw it. He was in the UK shooting a new version of the movie *Batman* at the time. He thought that the façade of the building would be perfect as the exterior of Wayne Manor, the home of Batman. But the inside of Wayne Manor was actually shot at another big house in the same area – Hatfield House.

The inside of Knebworth House has also been used in many movies. An important scene from the 2010 Oscar-winning movie *The King's Speech* was shot in the ballroom. This movie was made by the British director Tom Hooper. It starred Colin Firth as the young King George VI of England, who had a speech impediment. The ballroom was the venue for a party that was held by his older brother Edward. In a corner of the room, Edward tells George that he is planning to marry divorced American woman, Wallis Simpson, something that makes it impossible for him to be King of England. It is George who becomes King instead.

And, of course, like many other historic buildings in the UK, Knebworth has made an appearance in the Harry Potter movies. In the fourth movie of the series, *Harry Potter and the Goblet of Fire*, a holiday dance is held in Hogwarts School. Before the dancing starts, there is a scene where one of Harry's friends appears in a beautiful long dress. The staircase that she descends while her friends look on in amazement is, in fact, the one in Knebworth House.

These are just a few of the famous scenes filmed at Knebworth House. To discover more, why not visit Knebworth yourself? The house is only 27 miles from London, and is easy to get to by car or by train. Knebworth House is a must for all movie lovers visiting the UK.

b Read the text again. Mark the sentences T (true) or F (false).

1 Knebworth is a favorite destination for music lovers. _T_
2 The house isn't occupied anymore. ___
3 Many movies have been made at Knebworth. ___
4 Tim Burton used the outside of the house in one of his movies. ___
5 You can see the outside of the house in *The King's Speech*. ___
6 George VI makes an important announcement to all his guests at Knebworth. ___
7 Harry Potter walks down the staircase in Knebworth in one of the movies. ___
8 Knebworth House is not far from London. ___

c Look at the highlighted words and phrases. What do you think they mean? Use your dictionary to look up their meaning and pronunciation.

d Complete the sentences with one of the highlighted words or phrases.

1 My sister didn't really like the _new version_ of *Pride and Prejudice*. She prefers the old one.
2 Palaces often have a _____ where people come for a formal dance or party.
3 Nowadays, you can visit _____ _____ in the UK to see how very rich families lived in the past.
4 In the summer, I love going to _____-_____ concerts. It's more fun than going to an indoor concert.
5 A hotel near a beach is a popular _____ for weddings.
6 A person with a _____ _____ can find it very hard to speak in public.

5 LISTENING

a ONLINE Listen to a tour guide talking to a group before she takes them on the TV and Movie Walking Tour of Central Park in New York City. Number the places in the order she mentions them.

a a carousel ☐   e a hotel ☐
b a bridge 1   f a lake ☐
c a memorial ☐   g a fountain ☐
d a skating rink ☐

b Listen again and correct any mistakes in the sentences. Check (✓) the sentences that are correct.

1 The tour will last for three hours.
   two hours.
2 The Gapstow Bridge is made of wood.
   _____.
3 The Plaza Hotel was featured in *The Great Gatsby*.
   _____.
4 There is one skating rink in Central Park.
   _____.
5 The Carousel has 47 wooden horses to ride on.
   _____.
6 The Boathouse Restaurant is next to the smallest lake in Central Park.
   _____.
7 The Bow Bridge was used as a location in the TV show *Glee*.
   _____.
8 The last time sheep were in the Sheep Meadow was 1943.
   _____.

c Listen again with the audioscript on p. 73.

Wollman Skating Rink

the Carousel

Bow Bridge

USEFUL WORDS AND PHRASES

Learn these words and phrases.

alley /ˈæli/
aristocratic /əˈrɪstəkrætɪk/
gangsters /ˈgæŋstərz/
servants /ˈsərvənts/
tomb /tum/
fictional /ˈfɪkʃənl/
spectacular /spɛkˈtækyələr/
currently /ˈkərəntli/
on the edge of /ɑn ði ˈɛdʒ əv/

6B Judging by appearances

> What lies behind appearance is usually another appearance.
> *Mason Cooley, US writer*

1 VOCABULARY the body

a Label the picture.

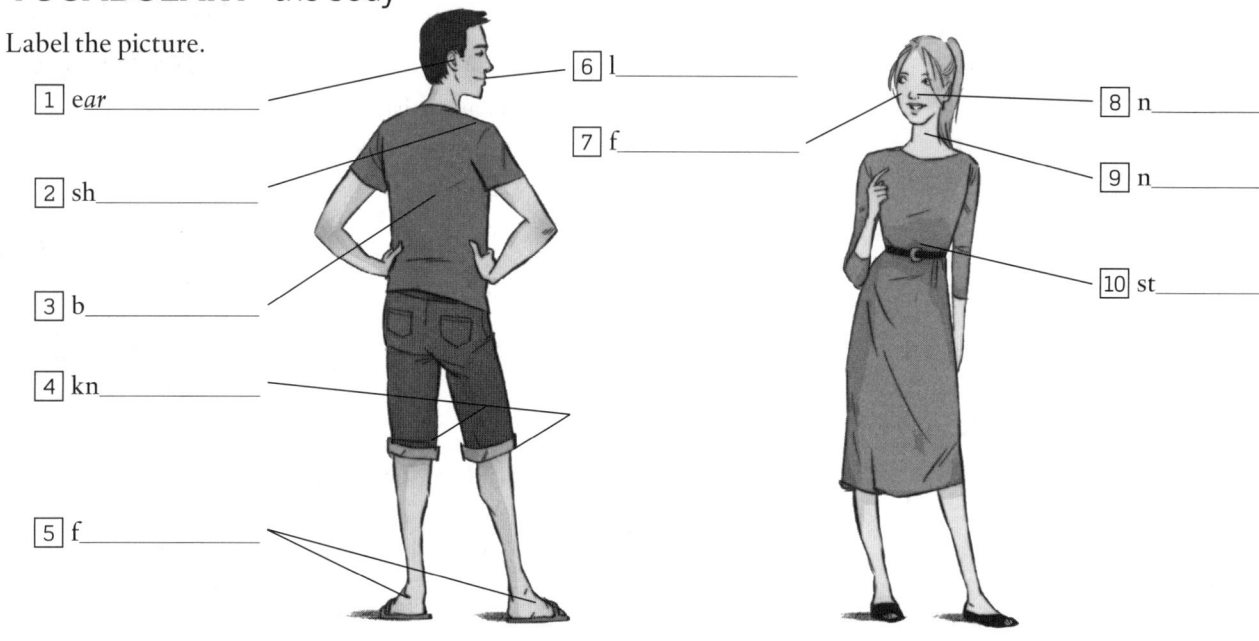

1 e*ar*
2 sh_____
3 b_____
4 kn_____
5 f_____
6 l_____
7 f_____
8 n_____
9 n_____
10 st_____

b Complete the sentences with the verbs in the box.

| bite | clap | kick | nod | point | smell | smile | ~~stare~~ |
| taste | touch | throw | whistle |

1 It's rude to _stare_ at people. It can make them feel uncomfortable.
2 You'll have to _____ the ball harder to score a goal.
3 Don't _____ the door – I just painted it.
4 Can you _____ the soup? I think it might need more salt.
5 I can _____ something burning. Did you turn off the oven?
6 When you're introduced to someone, you should _____, say hello, and shake hands.
7 We often _____ our heads when we agree with someone or understand what they said.
8 Did the audience _____ much at the end of the concert?
9 Lisa doesn't like dogs because she thinks they'll _____ her.
10 I often _____ a tune when I'm in the shower.
11 Don't drop your potato chip bag on the floor. _____ it in the trash.
12 When I'm abroad, it's sometimes easier to _____ at something I want in a store.

2 PRONUNCIATION diphthongs

a Circle the word with the different sound.

1 aɪ bike	bite smile height (weight)	
2 eɪ train	face great eyes taste	
3 oʊ phone	nose tongue throw toes	
4 aʊ owl	sound crowd mouth shoulders	
5 ɔɪ boy	point enjoy noise outgoing	

b ONLINE Listen and check. Then listen again and repeat the words.

3 GRAMMAR modals of deduction: might, can't, must

a Circle the correct answers.

1 That woman **can't** / must be the new manager. Our new manager is a man.

2 You *must* / *can't* be tired. You had a long trip.

3 They *must* / *can't* have much money. They never go out.

4 Don't buy Oliver a book. He *might not* / *must not* like the same kind of things as you.

5 Paula *can't* / *might* be injured. That's her best time ever for a marathon.

6 Your neighbor *must* / *might not* have a good job. Those cars are really expensive!

b Complete the sentences with *must, might, might not,* or *can't*.

1 He lived in Argentina for five years so he ___must___ speak Spanish well!
2 You _____ be very busy at work. You're always on Facebook!
3 I'm not sure, but Jenna _____ be on vacation. She didn't come to work today.
4 Mark passed all his final exams. His parents _____ be very proud.
5 Do you really think the US will win tonight? You _____ be serious! They have no chance!
6 Lucy wasn't feeling well this afternoon, so she _____ come to the party tonight. She said she would let us know later today.
7 I thought our neighbor was away for the weekend, but she _____ be – I just saw her in her yard.
8 It's very cold this evening and there are a lot of clouds. I think it _____ snow.

4 LISTENING

a **ONLINE** Listen to a radio program about the history of beauty. Check (✓) the three periods in history that the guest talks about.

1 ancient Greece ☐
2 the Egyptians ☐
3 the seventeenth century ☐
4 the Middle Ages ☐
5 the Romans ☐
6 the nineteenth century ☐

> **Glossary**
> *lead* = a soft, heavy, gray metal
> *powder* = a dry substance in the form of very small grains

b Listen again and mark the sentences T (true) or F (false).

1 Women and men wore makeup in ancient Egypt.   *T*
2 The Egyptians only wore black and white makeup.   __
3 Egyptian men wore makeup to protect their skin from the sun.   __
4 The Greeks thought that brown hair was the most beautiful.   __
5 Greek women used a substance that was dangerous in their makeup.   __
6 Beauty was very important to Roman people.   __
7 Roman women put their makeup on themselves.   __

c Listen again with the audioscript on p. 73.

5 READING

a Read the article once. What is the writer's opinion of Photoshopping?

1. Publishers should be able to use it as much as they want to. ☐
2. Publishers should be able to use it a little. ☐
3. Publishers shouldn't be able to use it at all. ☐

b Read the article again and choose the correct answers.

1. According to the article, publishers use Photoshopping to make people look…
   a. as good as possible.
   b. as interesting as possible.
   c. as thin as possible.
2. The article says that Photoshopped images have a bad effect on…
   a. girls of all ages.
   b. young teenagers.
   c. all kinds of people.
3. The new program gives a rating of 1 to an image with…
   a. no Photoshopping.
   b. a little Photoshopping.
   c. a lot of Photoshopping.
4. People complained about the Rachel Weisz ad because…
   a. it made her look a lot younger than she is.
   b. it showed the actress as she really is.
   c. it used an image of a different actress.
5. The people who will benefit most from the new tool are…
   a. advertisers.
   b. consumers.
   c. publishers.

c Look at the highlighted words and phrases. What do you think they mean? Use your dictionary to look up their meaning and pronunciation.

d Complete the sentences with one of the highlighted words or phrases.

1. Our neighbors are _relying_ on us to water their plants while they're away.
2. Animal rights groups want experiments on animals to be _____.
3. We're _____ our vacation plans so that we arrive on Thursday instead of Saturday.
4. I can't _____ _____ how to download this program.
5. In general, the older you get, the more _____ you have in your skin.
6. In most countries, movies are given a _____ to show which age group they are suitable for.

Photoshopping: how much is too much?

Today, it is normal for magazines to show pictures of models and celebrities that have been "Photoshopped." This means that the original photos have been changed on a computer using Photoshop® software to make them look better. The beautiful people in the photographs have perfect skin, no fat on their stomachs, and no wrinkles on their faces. They look so perfect and beautiful that what we see can't be real. But some publishers and advertisers insist that Photoshopping is necessary so that celebrities and models always look their best.

On the other hand, health organizations have warned that digitally altering photographs may be dangerous. They say Photoshopped images are not realistic, and may have a negative effect on people. Psychologists agree with the health organizations. They say some people try so hard to look like the pictures in magazines that they get sick. In some cases, they want to be as thin as the models and so they stop eating enough. When they realize that it is impossible to look so good, they get depressed. This doesn't only happen to young girls, but it can happen to people of all ages. So what can be done to keep everybody happy? Two researchers at Dartmouth University in New Hampshire, think they have found the answer.

Professor Hany Farid and Doctor Eric Klee have developed a computer program that can detect how much Photoshopping has been used on an image. Their software gives a rating from 1 to 5 to the image – 1 for a few changes, and 5 for a lot of changes. Farid and Klee's idea is that publishers include the rating next to the image. That way, consumers will be able to figure out how realistic the image is.

News of Farid and Klee's system has come out at the same time as people have started criticizing the use of Photoshopping. They say that some advertisers are going too far with it. Recently, the actress Rachel Weisz appeared in an ad for an anti-aging beauty cream. In the ad, Ms. Weisz looked like a teenager – in fact, she's in her early forties. There were a lot of complaints about the image and the ad was eventually banned. Farid and Klee's system could solve two problems at the same time. First, it would serve as a kind of health warning for consumers, and second, it may stop advertisers from relying on Photoshopping so much.

USEFUL WORDS AND PHRASES

Learn these words and phrases.

stage /steɪdʒ/	go viral /goʊ ˈvaɪrəl/
achieve /əˈtʃiv/	grow up /groʊ ˈʌp/
dye (hair) /daɪ/	take seriously /teɪk ˈsɪriəsli/
judge (vb) /dʒʌdʒ/	vitally important /ˈvaɪtli ɪmˈpɔrtnt/
carefree /ˈkɛrfri/	set an example /sɛt ən ɪɡˈzæmpl/

ONLINE FILE 6

7A Extraordinary school for boys

> Education is what survives when what has been learned has been forgotten.
> B. F. Skinner, US psychologist

1 VOCABULARY education

a Complete the sentences with the correct word.

In the US
1. A school for children aged from about two to five is a p_reschool._
2. A school for children aged from five to 10 is an el_____ school.
3. A school for children aged from 11 to 13 is a m_____ school.
4. A school for children aged from 13 to 18 is a h_____ school.
5. The class children are in is called a gr_____.
6. The school year is divided into two s_____.
7. Students have to apply to a c_____ before they can study there.

In the UK
8. A school for children aged from about two to five is a n_____ school.
9. A school for children aged from five to 11 is a pr_____ school.
10. A school for children aged from 11 to 18 is a s_____ school.
11. The person in charge of the school is the h_____ teacher.
12. The school year is divided into three t_____.
13. A school where children study, eat, and sleep is a b_____ school.
14. A person who goes on to study higher education usually studies at a u_____.

b Complete the sentences.
1. My friend was sick so she didn't t_ake_ the exam.
2. Some of the students in that class b_____ very badly.
3. If you ch_____ on the exam, the teacher won't grade it.
4. A boy was s_____ for stealing money from other students.
5. You'll f_____ your classes if you don't work harder.
6. I'm taking my driver's test tomorrow. I hope I p_____!
7. I have exams next week, so I'm going to s_____ this weekend.
8. The students were p_____ by the teacher for being noisy in class.

2 PRONUNCIATION the letter u

a Circle the word with a different sound.

1 boot	2 up	3 bull	4 /yu/
lunch	couple	cut	cute
fruit	mussels	full	musical
scooter	pull	push	subtitles
true	tongue	put	uniform

b ONLINE Listen and check. Then listen again and repeat the words.

3 GRAMMAR first conditional and future time clauses + *when*, *until*, etc.

a Match the sentence halves.

1. Joe's parents will be furious — c
2. As soon as I get my driver's license,
3. I'm sure we'll feel more relaxed
4. You'll have to go to a new school
5. He won't pass his test
6. Nina won't look for a job
7. I'll buy the book
8. If I don't feel well,

a. unless he studies more.
b. after we go on vacation.
c. if he fails his exam again.
d. before classes start.
e. I'm going to buy a car.
f. when your family moves to a new house.
g. I'll stay in bed.
h. until her daughter starts school.

43

b Complete the sentences with a word from the box.

| if | until | ~~when~~ | after | unless | before |

1 They won't have to wear a uniform _when_ they go to high school.
2 I won't leave early _____ the teacher gives me permission.
3 Ella will be disappointed _____ she doesn't get good test scores.
4 I'll take a long vacation _____ classes end.
5 The teacher won't start the class _____ all the students are quiet.
6 I'll talk to my teachers _____ I choose which colleges to apply to.

c Complete the sentences with the correct form of the verbs in parentheses. Use the simple present or future (will / won't).

1 I_'ll do_ do my homework as soon as I _get_ home. (do, get)
2 We _____ late unless we _____. (be, hurry up)
3 My friends _____ a going-away party before they _____ to Korea. (have, go)
4 The bus _____ for you if you _____ on time. (not wait, not be)
5 If the teacher _____, we _____ the exam. (not come, not take)
6 James _____ home until he _____ a job. (not leave, find)
7 Alice _____ buy a car unless her parents _____ her the money. (not be able to, lend)
8 As soon as my boyfriend _____ his test scores, he _____ me. (get, call)
9 She _____ kindergarten until she _____ five years old. (not start, be)
10 You _____ better if you _____ every day. (play, practice)

4 READING

a Read the article once. What do South Korean students do in a *hagwon*?

1 sleep ☐   3 study ☐
2 meet friends ☐   4 have lunch ☐

When is it time to stop studying?

It's 10 p.m. and six government employees are out checking the streets of Seoul, South Korea. But these are not police officers looking for teenagers who are behaving badly. Their mission is to find children who are still studying. And stop them.

Education in South Korea is very competitive. The aim of almost every schoolchild is to get into one of the country's top universities. Only the students with the best grades get a place. The school day starts at 8 a.m. and students finish studying somewhere between 10 p.m. and 1 a.m. at night. This is because many go to private academies called *hagwon* after school. Around 74 percent of all students attend a hagwon after their regular classes finish. A year's course costs, on average, $2,600 per student. In Seoul, there are more private tutors than schoolteachers, and the most popular ones make millions of dollars a year from online and in-person classes. Most parents rely on private tutoring to get their children into a university.

With so much time spent in the classroom, all that students in South Korean high schools do is study and sleep. Some of them are so exhausted that they cannot stay awake the next day at school. It is a common sight to see a teacher explaining the lesson while a third of the students are asleep on their desks. The teachers don't seem to mind. There are even special pillows for sale that fit over the arms of the chairs to make sleeping in class more comfortable. Ironically, the students spend class time sleeping so that they can stay up late studying that night.

The South Korean government has been aware of the faults in the system for some time, but now they have passed some reforms. Today, schoolteachers have to meet certain standards or take additional training courses.

However, the biggest challenge for the government is the hagwons. Hagwons have been banned from having classes after 10 p.m., which is why there are street patrols looking for children who are studying after that time. If they find any in class, the owner of the hagwon is punished and the students are sent home. It's a strange world, where some children have to be told to stop studying while others are reluctant to start.

b Read the article again. Mark the sentences T (true) or F (false).

1. The street patrol in Seoul is looking for criminals.   _F_
2. Most students in South Korea want to go to a university.   ___
3. All private tutors in South Korea are paid well.   ___
4. Schoolteachers are used to students who sleep in class.   ___
5. The government is doing nothing to improve the education system.   ___
6. Every academy must close before 9 p.m.   ___
7. Students are punished if they are found in a *hagwon*.   ___

c Look at the highlighted words and phrases. What do you think they mean? Use your dictionary to look up their meaning and pronunciation.

d Complete the sentences with one of the highlighted words or phrases from the text.

1. It's a real _challenge_ for teachers to get all their students to pass their exams.
2. Jon hurt his neck, so he shouldn't use two _____ in bed.
3. It's very _____ to get into some universities. You need excellent grades.
4. My children are _____ to go outside when it's cold.
5. People using laptops on the bus is a _____ _____ these days.
6. Mary needed extra help with math and history, so she has private _____ to help her with these subjects.

5 LISTENING

a ONLINE Listen to a radio program about a new TV series. Which word describes the methods used by the teacher in the series?

1. unusual   ☐
2. traditional   ☐
3. old-fashioned   ☐

b Listen again and correct the mistakes.

1. The series is a **drama**.
   reality show
2. The students are **sixteen**.
   _____
3. A boy says he'll burn a **car**.
   _____
4. The teacher used to be a **soldier**.
   _____
5. He teaches **math** at a high school.
   _____
6. The students have to say **a number** in the game.
   _____
7. The students read Shakespeare to some **dogs**.
   _____
8. The punctuation lesson is in a **classroom**.
   _____
9. Some of the students think the teacher is **crazy**.
   _____
10. The next episode is the following **Friday**.
    _____

c Listen again with the audioscript on p.74.

USEFUL WORDS AND PHRASES

Learn these words and phrases.

a prodigy /ə ˈprɑdədʒi/
determined (to do something) /dɪˈtərmənd/
resent (somebody) /rɪˈzɛnt/
take up (tennis) /ˈteɪk ʌp/
required /rɪˈkwaɪərd/
forbidden /fərˈbɪdn/
outstanding /aʊtˈstændɪŋ/
prestigious /prɛˈstɪdʒəs/
cause controversy /kɔz ˈkɑntrəˌvəsi/
push (somebody) too hard /pʊʃ tu ˈhɑrd/

7B Ideal home

> Home is a place you grow up wanting to leave and grow old wanting to get back to.
> John Ed Pearce, US journalist

1 GRAMMAR second conditional

a Match the sentence halves.

1. If we had the time, — *d*
2. I would like my apartment more
3. Luke would be able to get a job in Tokyo
4. If my sister didn't work so hard,
5. If we bought a bigger house in the suburbs,
6. If they could live anywhere they wanted to,
7. We'd have more privacy
8. I wouldn't want to live in New York City,

a she could spend more time with her children.
b they'd move to California.
c if he could speak better Japanese.
d ~~we'd do the housework ourselves.~~
e if we didn't have to share an apartment.
f unless I earned a lot of money.
g if it were on the top floor.
h we'd be able to have a dog.

b Complete the sentences with the correct form of the verbs in parentheses. Use the second conditional.

1. If I _had_ more time, _I'd paint_ my room myself. (have, paint)
2. Lucy's room _____ better organized if she _____ it more often. (be, clean)
3. I _____ my car to work if I _____ a parking space. (not take, not have)
4. _____ you _____ your job if you _____ a lot of money? (keep, win)
5. Jack _____ his mother every day if he _____ a girlfriend. (not call, have)
6. We _____ so often if our stove _____ broken. (not eat out, not be)
7. If I _____ a big argument with my neighbors because of a problem, I _____ away. (have, not move)
8. If our house _____ so small, you _____ all stay the night. (not be, can)
9. _____ you _____ if you _____ your alarm? (wake up, not set)
10. If we _____ another bathroom, there _____ a line for the shower. (have, not be)

2 PRONUNCIATION sentence stress

a ONLINE Listen and complete the sentences.

1. If I _exercised_ more, I'd be a lot healthier.
2. I'd _____ my own _____ if I had a garden.
3. Would you _____ a _____ if you had enough money?
4. If it were my house, I _____ _____ the kitchen bigger.
5. I _____ _____ so hard if I didn't have pay so much rent.

b Listen again and repeat the sentences. <u>Copy</u> the <u>rhy</u>thm.

c Match the words with the same sounds.

1. c**o**sy — a s**u**burb
2. c**ei**ling — b k**i**tchen
3. t**ow**n — c w**a**lkway
4. c**ou**ntry — d sh**ow**er
5. sp**a**cious — e gr**ou**nd
6. balc**o**ny — f b**a**sement

d ONLINE Listen and check. Then listen again and repeat the words.

3 VOCABULARY houses

a Complete the sentences with *in* or *on* and a phrase from the box.

| the fourth floor | the outskirts | ~~a suburb~~ |
| the West Coast | the woods | |

1. We're looking at apartments outside of the city. We want to live _in a suburb_.
2. Sara bought a small cabin _____ because she loves looking at the birds and trees.
3. Here's your key. Your room is _____.
4. I'd love to live by the ocean, maybe _____.
5. Chris lives _____ of the city, so he has to commute downtown every day.

b Complete the ads.

FOR RENT

This ¹m_odern_ apartment is on the ²t_____ fl_____ of a building with magnificent views of the Charles River. It has three bedrooms, a bathroom, and a large ³sp_____ kitchen. The living room has a ⁴w_____ fl_____ and there is carpet in all the bedrooms. There is a large ⁵b_____ outside the living room with space for a table, chairs, and plants. There is a garage in the ⁶b_____ with room for two cars.

This old-fashioned ⁷c_____ is situated on a quiet mountain road. It has a kitchen, living room, and two small, but ⁸c_____ bedrooms. All the rooms have low ⁹c_____ , and the walls are made of ¹⁰l_____. There is a ¹¹f_____ in the living room, but the house also has central heat. There is a small ¹²d_____ on the side of the house with a pretty view of the mountains. Several beautiful stone ¹³s_____ lead to the front ¹⁴e_____ of the house.

4 LISTENING

a **ONLINE** Listen to a guide giving a tour of Elvis Presley's home, Graceland. Number the places and parts of the house in the order you hear about them.

a TV room ☐   e dining room ☐
b music room ☐ f basement ☐
c living room ☐ g the walls ☐
d the front door ☐1☐

b Listen again and answer the questions.

1 When was the house built?
  In the early twentieth century.
2 How long did Elvis Presley live in Graceland?
  _____
3 When did he get married?
  _____
4 How many children did he have?
  _____
5 How many TVs did Elvis Presley have in the TV room?
  _____
6 At what time did Elvis Presley usually wake up?
  _____
7 Other than eating meals, what did Elvis Presley like to do in the dining room?
  _____
8 On what floor did Elvis Presley's parents have a room?
  _____

c Listen again with the audioscript on p. 74.

5 READING

a Read the article once and choose the best title for it.

1. Top tips on buying a new house ☐
2. Finding out where you really live ☐
3. The most interesting houses to visit in London ☐

1 _D_
Are you interested in the history of your house? If you are, then you might want to get in touch with a house historian. A house historian's job is to find out what has happened to a particular house in the past. They try to discover who built the house, who has lived in the building since it was built, and what was on the site of the building before. Their research can uncover all kinds of interesting information.

2 ___
We spoke to house historian Tracy Collins, who told us some of her stories. One of the houses she had to research was an apartment at 200 Oxford Street in London. She discovered that the author George Orwell had once stayed with the owners of the apartment. He had slept in the smallest bedroom in the apartment, which was very dark. Later, when he wrote his novel *1984*, he used the room as the inspiration for the famous Room 101. On another occasion, she was looking into the story of an apartment building in Orchard Court, also in London. She found out that the apartment had been used by spies during the World War II. First of all, the spies were invited to the building for a job interview. If they were successful, they took a training course. After the course, they returned to the apartment for their instructions. Then, they were sent on a mission. But Tracy's third story is even more dramatic. When she was investigating a house in another part of London, she discovered that a murder had happened there!

3 ___
However, house historians do not only focus on one particular house. They also find out about the area where the house was built. Some areas are completely different now than they were in the past. One example is an area in Central London called Belgravia. Today, it is one of the richest neighborhoods in the world, but in the early nineteenth century, it was a poorer area. People used to go there during the day to hang their laundry or to collect plants for food. At night, many people would avoid the area because it was full of criminals.

4 ___
If you can't afford to pay a professional to research the history of your house, you can try to research the past yourself. The best place to start is to find all the official documents belonging to your house. These should give you some idea of who the previous owners were. After that, you should go to the office that has the official documents of your area. Some of these go back hundreds of years! You may not find out anything particularly interesting about your house, but you'll definitely to enjoy the search.

b Match the headings with the paragraphs in the article. There are two extra headings that you do not need to use.

A What was there before?
B How much do house historians charge?
C How can you do it yourself?
~~D What does a house historian do?~~
E What do you need to become a house historian?
F What has one house historian discovered?

c Look at the highlighted words and phrases. What do you think they mean? Use your dictionary to look up their meaning and pronunciation.

d Complete the sentences with one of the highlighted words or phrases.

1. The police are _looking_ _into_ a robbery at the school.
2. I'm going to _____ my family history.
3. Some of the houses in this town _____ _____ to the seventeenth century.
4. I didn't paint my living room. It was done by the _____ owner of the house.
5. When the washing machine finishes, can you _____ the clothes to dry, please?
6. You should always read the _____ before you try to build a bookcase.

USEFUL WORDS AND PHRASES

Learn these words and phrases.

bookcase /ˈbʊkkeɪs/
property /ˈprɑpərti/
tower /ˈtaʊər/
hang (a picture) /hæŋ/
overlook (sth) /oʊvərˈlʊk/
remain /rɪˈmeɪn/
settle (in a village) /ˈsetl/
plain /pleɪn/
peace and quiet /pis ən ˈkwaɪət/
turn into /tərn ˈɪntə/

ONLINE FILE 7

Practical English Boys' night out

1 MAKING SUGGESTIONS

Complete the dialogue with the words in the box.

could	Let's	great	going	about	go
don't	feel				

Jess I'm hungry. Where should we ¹ _go_ for lunch?
Phil I think there's a burger place near here. ² _____ go there.
Jess Phil, you know I don't eat meat.
Phil Oops! Sorry, I forgot. How about ³ _____ to that Italian place you like?
Jess Aren't you on a diet?
Phil Well, yes. But we ⁴ _____ order a salad.
Jess No, thanks. I don't ⁵ _____ like a salad today. Why ⁶ _____ we try that new sushi restaurant?
Phil I'd rather not. I'm not crazy about raw fish.
Jess Well, what ⁷ _____ having some Chinese? I know a really good place.
Phil That's a ⁸ _____ idea. Where is it?

2 SOCIAL ENGLISH

Complete the dialogue.

Ellie Joe?
Joe Hi, Ellie.
Ellie It's Mom's birthday, and you're late. Where are you, ¹ a_nyway_?
Joe That's ² w_____ I'm calling. I'm not going to ³ m_____ it for dinner.
Ellie Why not?
Joe I'm at my sister's house. She's ⁴ o_____ to Miami tomorrow to start her new job and I wanted to say goodbye.
Ellie But why tonight? It's ⁵ n_____ that I don't think you should say goodbye, but couldn't you do it tomorrow?
Joe Not really. I wanted to have a ⁶ w_____ with her about something before she left.
Ellie Mom's going to be upset.
Joe Sorry, Ellie. It won't ⁷ h_____ again. I'll call you tomorrow.

3 READING

a Read the text and answer the questions.

1 Where can you get a map of New York?
  From the Visitor Information Center.
2 How much is a seven-day MetroCard? _____
3 What is the best time to visit the Empire State Building? _____
4 How many islands do you visit on the Statue of Liberty tour? _____
5 What time does the bike tour around Central Park leave? _____
6 What day can you visit MoMA in the evening? _____

What to do in New York

To explore New York, you'll need a map and a MetroCard. Maps are available at the Visitor Information Center and you can buy a MetroCard at any of the subway stations. A seven-day pass costs $30, and you can use it on the subways and city buses. Below are some places you might like to visit.

Empire State Building
Take an elevator to the 86th floor to get the best views of the city. Come at 8:30 a.m. to avoid the crowds, or try visiting during lunch and dinner hours from Monday to Wednesday when it's quieter. An adult ticket is $25, or you can get an express pass for $50. Buy your ticket online to reduce your time standing in line.

Statue of Liberty
This famous New York landmark is only accessible by ferry. You should get your tickets in advance either online, by phone, or in person at the ferry departure points. An adult ticket costs $24 and includes a tour of Liberty Island and a visit to the Immigration Museum on Ellis Island.

Central Park
Central Park is very big, so the best way to see it is by bike. It costs $20 to rent one for two hours and ride around the park on your own, or you can book a tour, which costs about $47 per person. The tour leaves daily at 9 a.m.

MoMA
MoMA is the most influential museum of modern art in the world, so it's definitely worth a visit. There are famous works by Picasso, Kandinsky, Andy Warhol, and many, many more. It is open from 10 a.m. to 5:30 p.m. (8 p.m. on Fridays) and tickets are $25 for adults.

b Underline five words or phrases you don't know. Use your dictionary to look up their meaning and pronunciation.

8A Sell and tell

> I always say shopping is cheaper than a psychiatrist.
> Tammy Faye Bakker, US TV host

1 VOCABULARY shopping

a Complete the sentences.
 1 We always book our flights on_line_.
 2 We spent all day checking out the different stores at the m_____.
 3 Are you sure that jacket f_____ you?
 4 My sister buys all her clothes at an ou_____ st_____ because it's cheaper.
 5 There was a line at the b_____ st_____ because all the novels were half price.
 6 That's a beautiful shirt. Why don't you t_____ it o_____?
 7 They went to the ph_____ to buy some aspirin.
 8 That store is having a s_____. All winter coats are 20% off.
 9 I wouldn't buy that dress, if I were you. It doesn't s_____ you.
 10 The sports section is on the top floor of the d_____ st_____.

making nouns from verbs

b Complete the text with the noun form of the verbs in parentheses.

> A month ago, I bought a video game online for my son's birthday. They sent me an order confirmation saying that ¹ _delivery_ (deliver) would take about ten days. Two weeks later I began to worry. The seller had received my ² _____ (pay), but the video game had not arrived. So I decided to make a ³ _____ (complain). I sent an email to the seller with a copy of the order confirmation as an ⁴ _____ (attach). I received a ⁵ _____ (respond) immediately saying that the seller would look into the incident. After that, I heard nothing for three days, so I sent another email demanding an ⁶ _____ (explain). This time I had more ⁷ _____ (succeed) and the seller said he would send another copy of the game. If I don't receive it before my son's birthday, I'm going to ask for ⁸ _____ (compensate).

2 GRAMMAR reported speech: sentences and questions

a Circle the correct answer. Check (✓) if both are correct.
 1 Matt said yesterday that he *will* / *would* come shopping.
 2 We asked the salesperson how much *it was* / *was it*.
 3 My sister *said me* / *told me* that she had spent all her money at the sale.
 4 I asked Lucy where *she bought* / *did she buy* her clothes.
 5 You told me that you *may* / *might* go shopping on Saturday.
 6 My brother asked me *if I can* / *if I could* lend him some money to buy a new video game.
 7 Kate said that she *had to* / *must* go to the supermarket.
 8 I asked my sister *whether* / *that* the dress suited me, and she said I looked great!
 9 Carolina asked me what *I wanted* / *did I want* from the mall.
 10 Nick said that he couldn't pay me back, because he *has forgotten* / *had forgotten* his wallet.

b Change the direct speech into reported sentences and questions.

 1 I haven't been to the sale yet.
 2 I hate buying clothes.
 3 How much did you pay for your jacket?
 4 I'll check the price online.
 5 Where's the shoe department?
 6 Does the shirt fit you?

 1 Jackie said _(that) she hadn't been to the sale yet_.
 2 My boyfriend told me _____.
 3 They asked me _____.
 4 You said _____.
 5 I asked her _____.
 6 The salesperson asked me _____.

50

3 READING

a Read the article once and match the headings with the paragraphs.

A Check out the company you are buying from
B Keep copies of all documents
C Check the terms and conditions of the seller
D Check your computer before and after buying online
E ~~Always use a credit card~~
F Be security-conscious

b Look at the highlighted words and phrases. What do you think they mean? Use your dictionary to look up their meaning and pronunciation.

c Complete the sentences with one of the highlighted words or phrases.

1 I don't understand people who stand in line all night just to buy the most _up-to-date_ smartphones.
2 You should change your passwords frequently so that _____ can't get into your computer.
3 I put a _____ on the garage door to protect my car.
4 My friend said she would meet me outside the movie theater, but she didn't _____ _____.
5 I forgot to _____ _____ of Facebook, and my boss read my messages.
6 Some people don't bother with a _____ these days – they only have a smartphone.

Top tips for safe online shopping

US shoppers spent $202 billion buying items online in 2011. Experts predict that our spending will increase to $327 billion by 2016. Read on to find out how you can protect yourself when you are shopping online.

1 _E_
When you buy things on the Internet, there is always a chance that something may go wrong. The product could be broken when you get it, or it might not turn up at all. If this happens, your credit card will offer you the best protection. Some credit cards allow you to dispute a purchase, meaning the credit card company will stop payment on a purchase until the matter is resolved. This is why a credit card is the best way to pay.

2 __
Make sure that your device, for example your laptop or tablet, is safe to use at all times. It should be protected by up-to-date antivirus software, and you should also install a personal firewall, which will stop hackers from attacking your system. Make sure that your firewall is turned on before you start shopping, and when you finish be sure to log out of the system, especially if you share your computer with other people.

3 __
Take a minute to look at the website before you buy anything. Check that the company has a geographical address as well as a landline telephone number, and write down these details. It is generally better to use sellers that you know about or ones that have been recommended to you.

4 __
Somewhere on the seller's website, there should be a list of all your rights (for example, what to do if you have a problem with the item you bought, or if it hasn't arrived). Make sure you read this before you decide to shop there. If you can't find the list, you should probably choose a different website.

5 __
A special icon on your screen will tell you if the website you are using is safe. The icon is in the shape of a padlock, and you can find it on the browser bar at the top or bottom of the screen. Another indication of a safe website is its address. The address should begin with "https" and not "http" – the **s** stands for secure.

6 __
The final stage of online shopping is the order confirmation. This is proof that you have bought a product from this company, and it contains the special reference number for your order. You should always print this information and keep it somewhere safe – you might need it if there is a problem.

4 PRONUNCIATION the letters *ai*

a Circle the word where ***ai*** is pronounced differently.

1 barg**ai**n	vill**ai**n	(**pai**d)
2 cert**ai**n	compl**ai**n	r**ai**n
3 p**ai**nting	s**ai**d	w**ai**t
4 **ai**rline	f**ai**r	r**ai**se
5 capt**ai**n	pl**ai**n	em**ai**l
6 br**ai**n	h**ai**r	st**ai**rs

b **ONLINE** Listen and check. Then listen again and repeat the words.

5 LISTENING

a **ONLINE** Listen to a conversation about a complaint. Answer the questions.

1 Where was Sam flying to when he had a problem?

_____

2 How many emails did Sam send to the Airline?

_____

b Listen again and choose the correct answers.

1 Sam usually pays for Preferred Access because…
   a he's always late for flights.
   (b) he hates waiting in line.
   c he's really scared of flying.
   d he likes sitting by the window.
2 Sam's problem at the airport was…
   a there wasn't any space left for baggage.
   b he'd forgotten to take his passport.
   c he didn't get the service he'd paid for.
   d there was a long line at the check-in desk.
3 In Sam's first email…
   a he complained about the airline staff.
   b he said the airline should stop Preferred Access.
   c he asked the airline for a small amount of money.
   d he told the airline he would never fly with them again.
4 The man who replied to the first email…
   a didn't offer to give Sam any money.
   b took a long time to write back.
   c said he would send Sam a check for $20.
   d didn't believe Sam's story.
5 The result of Sam's complaint was that…
   a the airline gave him two free flights.
   b he got exactly what he asked for.
   c he will never use the airline again.
   d the airline gave him more than he asked for.

c Listen again with the audioscript on p. 74.

USEFUL WORDS AND PHRASES

Learn these words and phrases.

hesitate /ˈhɛzəteɪt/
refund (vb) /rɪˈfʌnd/
slip (vb) /slɪp/
spoil /spɔɪl/
swear /swɛr/
faulty /ˈfɔlti/
a satisfied customer /ə sætəsfaɪd ˈkʌstəmər/
make (sth) clear /meɪk klɪr/
get into an argument /gɛt ˈɪntu ən ˈɑrgyəmənt/
waste your time /weɪst yər taɪm/

People who work sitting down get paid more than people who work standing up.

Ogden Nash, US poet

8B What's the right job for you?

1 VOCABULARY work

a Complete the text with a word from the box.

| applied | downsized | self-employed | ~~overtime~~ | promoted |
| resign | retire | set | shifts | training |

My father's first job was in a small local company. He had to work a lot of ¹ _overtime_, which he really hated. One day, he decided to ² _____ from the job. He ³ _____ for a new job with a multinational company. At first, he worked ⁴ _____ in a factory. Then, he was ⁵ _____ to supervisor. Later, he was ⁶ _____ because business was bad. After that, my dad took a ⁷ _____ course in business management, and he ⁸ _____ up his own business. He really enjoyed being ⁹ _____—he was his own boss so he could make all the rules! He didn't ¹⁰ _____ until he was 65 years old. This photo shows the party they gave him on his last day.

b Complete the sentences with a noun form of the word in **bold**.

1 A _musician_ plays **music** for a living.
2 They're looking for a _____ to **translate** some documents into Chinese.
3 The company **employs** over 200 people – 150 of whom have full-time _____.
4 Hanna studied **pharmacy** because she wanted to be a _____.
5 When we **retire**, we'd like to spend our _____ with our grandchildren.
6 They're going to **promote** someone, but we don't know who's going to get the _____.
7 Ken got a **law** degree because he wanted to be a _____.
8 My son is studying **science** because he wants to be a _____.
9 My colleague tried to **resign**, but our boss wouldn't accept his _____.
10 I **applied** for the job, but I sent in the _____ too late.
11 A _____ has to get up early to take care of his **farm**.
12 He wasn't **qualified** for the job, because he didn't have the right _____.

c Complete the sentences with the correct words.

1 My niece is still _in_ school, but she has a _part-time_ job on Friday nights and Saturdays.
2 Oliver is _____ his third year of college, but he hopes to get a _____ job for the summer. He'll work until the end of August.
3 My boyfriend works _____ a multinational company. He's _____ charge _____ human resources.
4 Dan got a Ph.D when he was _____ college. Now, he's very _____ _____.
5 Teresa has a _____ job. She works from 8 a.m. to 6 p.m. every day. Her job is _____, so she hopes to stay there until she retires.
6 My cousin didn't use to have a job, so he was _____. Now he's _____-_____ and he really enjoys working for himself.

53

2 PRONUNCIATION word stress

a Underline the stressed syllable.

1 a|pply
2 down|size
3 em|ploy|ment
4 far|mer
5 law|yer
6 o|ver|time
7 mu|si|cian
8 per|ma|nent
9 pro|mo|tion
10 qua|li|fy
11 re|sign
12 re|tire
13 sa|la|ry
14 tem|po|ra|ry
15 un|em|ployed

b **ONLINE** Listen and check. Then listen again and repeat.

3 GRAMMAR gerunds and infinitives

a Circle the correct answer.
1 She's going to practice *giving* / *to give* her presentation.
2 My colleague isn't very good at *making* / *to make* decisions.
3 Did they promise *paying* / *to pay* you on time?
4 The government is trying to make it easier for companies *firing* / *to fire* employees.
5 My brother regrets *not going* / *not to go* to college.
6 Can you remember *having* / *to have* your first job interview?
7 He really enjoys *working* / *to work* on a team.
8 Don't forget *signing* / *to sign* the application form.

b Correct any mistakes in the highlighted verbs. Check (✓) if the sentence is correct.
1 It isn't easy finding a good job these days.
   to find
2 My brother has decided to resign from his job.
   _____
3 I'd like getting a job abroad, preferably in Canada.
   _____
4 She spent three months to take a training course.
   _____
5 They'll have to increase the salary to attract the right applicants.
   _____
6 He gave up to play basketball when he went to college.
   _____
7 The interviewer asked me to wait in the reception area.
   _____
8 Fill out an application form can take a long time.
   _____

c Complete the sentences with the gerund or the infinitive form of the verbs in parentheses.
1 I forgot _to tell_ my boss I was going to the doctor's. (tell)
2 My girlfriend told me _____ her outside the movie theater. (meet)
3 _____ heavy weights can give you back problems. (lift)
4 It's always difficult _____ good seats if we don't get to the theater early. (find)
5 They're afraid of _____ fired. (get)
6 Why don't you try _____ to a smaller company? (apply)
7 My colleague doesn't mind _____ me with my problems. (help)
8 I can't afford _____ a lower salary. (accept)

4 READING

a Read the article once. Which job / jobs require a special qualification?

Do something different and get a super salary!

Would you like your friends to be impressed by your job? Do you want to earn a better salary? Here are some of the strangest jobs around that pay over $100,000 per year.

A Ethical hacker

What they do
A hacker doesn't usually have permission to enter a company's computer system. But an ethical hacker is actually employed by a company to take care of the system. Ethical hackers have to protect a company's IT network from real hackers. Their job is to stop professional criminals from entering the company's system to steal confidential information.

How to get a job
After getting a degree in IT, you have to work in computers for a few years until you have enough experience in programming. After that, you need to get a special qualification called the Certified Ethical Hacker (CEH) certificate, which lets you work as an ethical hacker. Salaries start between $50,000 and $100,000, depending on your experience and where you work.

B Golf-ball diver

What they do
Not all of the golf balls on a golf course end up in the hole on the green. In fact, golfers hit a surprisingly high number of them into the lake. Golf-ball divers do exactly what the job title suggests: they dive into the lake to collect the balls. Professional divers only work during the day. They have to wear special diving equipment, as well as a pair of thick waterproof gloves to keep their hands from getting cold.

How to get a job
To be a golf-ball diver, you need an advanced certificate in scuba diving. Once you have the right qualifications, you can choose to work for a company or to work for yourself. If you work for a company, the company will organize your schedule for you, whereas if you're self-employed, you have to contact the golf courses yourself. Golf-ball divers are paid between seven and 12 cents per ball, and on an average day, they can collect about 4,000 balls. If you work from 7 a.m. to noon four days a week, you can earn up to $100,000 per year.

C Forensic dentist

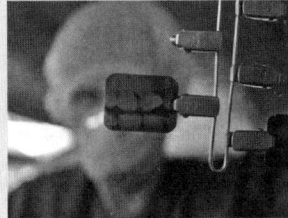

What they do
Forensic dentists spend most of their time identifying dead bodies. When a body is found, the dentist looks at the teeth and checks the records of other dentists to try and discover who the person was. If they don't find any information to match the dead person's teeth, the forensic dentist has to build up a profile about them. This profile contains information such as the person's sex, age, height, weight, and diet. Forensic dentists often work closely with the police and they sometimes have to give evidence in court.

How to get a job
First, you need to get a degree in dentistry and after that, you can take a postgraduate course to become a forensic dentist. You have to work in a laboratory for many years until you are promoted to department head. The starting salary is between $69,000 to $146,000 per year, but forensic dentists who go to court can earn up to $180,000.

b Read the article again. Answer the questions with the letters A, B, or C.

In which profession does the employee…?
1 work outside   *B*
2 try to stop a crime   ___
3 take part in criminal investigations   ___
4 need two degrees   ___
5 get paid depending on the results of a day's work   ___
6 do something that could be illegal   ___

c Look at the highlighted words and phrases. What do you think they mean? Use your dictionary to look up their meaning and pronunciation.

5 LISTENING

a **ONLINE** Listen to five speakers talking about their first job. Check (✓) the speakers who enjoyed their jobs and put an ✗ if they didn't enjoy them.

Speaker 1 ✓   Speaker 4 ☐
Speaker 2 ☐   Speaker 5 ☐
Speaker 3 ☐

b Listen again and mark the sentences T (true) or F (false).
1 Speaker 1 was downsized after three years.   *F*
2 Speaker 2 went abroad when he was a student.   ___
3 Speaker 3 didn't earn any money doing the job.   ___
4 Speaker 4 got along well with his colleagues.   ___
5 Speaker 5 wasn't wearing the right clothes for the job.   ___

c Listen again with the audioscript on p. 75.

USEFUL WORDS AND PHRASES

Learn these words and phrases.

entrepreneurs /ɑntrəprə'nərz/
a product /ə 'prɑdʌkt/
be successful /bi sək'sɛsfl/
impressive /ɪm'prɛsɪv/
profitable /'prɑfətəbl/
to make it /tə 'meɪk ɪt/
make a presentation /meɪk ə prɛzn'teɪʃn/
reject somebody's idea /rɪ'dʒɛkt aɪdɪə/
share the profits /ʃɛr ðə 'prɑfəts/

ONLINE FILE 8

> We must believe in luck. For how else can we explain the success of those we don't like?
>
> Jean Cocteau, French writer and artist

9A Lucky encounters

1 GRAMMAR third conditional

a Complete the sentences with the correct form of the verbs in parentheses.

1. If you'd told me you weren't hungry, I _wouldn't have made_ any dinner. (make)
2. They _____ on time if the train hadn't broken down. (arrive)
3. If he _____ his keys, he wouldn't have gone back home. (not forget)
4. You would have seen my message if you _____ your cell phone. (check)
5. I _____ the flight if the plane hadn't been delayed. (miss)
6. If you'd concentrated on what you were doing, you _____ so many mistakes. (not make)
7. If I'd known it was going to snow, I _____ a coat. (wear)
8. We _____ Joe if we'd known you didn't like him. (not invite)

b Complete the second sentence so that it means the same as the first.

1. I got to the restaurant late because I went to the wrong place first.
   If I hadn't gone to the wrong place first, _I wouldn't have gotten to the restaurant late_.
2. They called us because they had a problem.
   They wouldn't have called us _____.
3. Helen didn't have the right qualifications so she didn't get the job.
   If Helen had had the right qualifications, _____.
4. Alex wasn't very careful with his glasses, so he broke them.
   If Alex had been more careful with his glasses, _____.
5. You got lost because you didn't follow my directions.
   You wouldn't have gotten lost _____.
6. We didn't play tennis this afternoon because it was windy.
   If it hadn't been so windy this afternoon, _____.

2 PRONUNCIATION sentence stress

a **ONLINE** Listen and complete the sentences.

1. We'd have gotten to the movie theater on time if we'd _taken_ a _taxi_.
2. If you'd _____ me about the _____, I'd have gone.
3. She would have bought the coat if it _____ been so _____.
4. If I'd _____ you were _____, I wouldn't have called.
5. If they _____ _____ so badly in the second half, they would have won the game.
6. The flight would have been cheaper if we'd _____ last _____.

b Listen again and repeat the sentences. Copy the rhythm.

3 VOCABULARY making adjectives and adverbs

a Complete the chart with the two adjective forms of each noun in the box.

care ~~comfort~~ fortune luck patience

	+	−
adjective ending in -able	1 _comfortable_	2 _uncomfortable_
adjective ending in -ate	3 _____	4 _____
adjective ending in -ful / -less	5 _____	6 _____
adjective ending in -ient	7 _____	8 _____
adjective ending in -y	9 _____	10 _____

56

b Complete the text with the correct adjective or adverb of the nouns in parentheses.

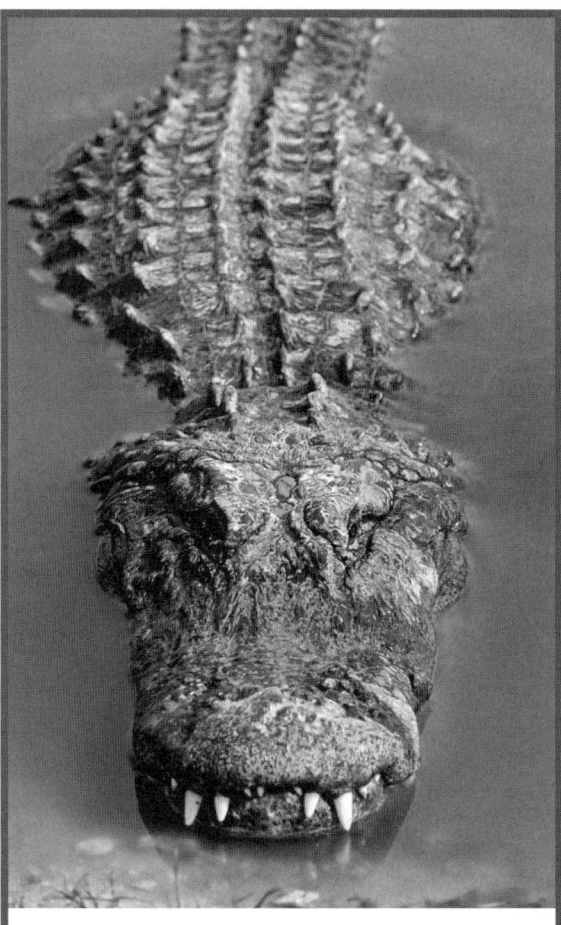

An American teenager made a [1] _careless_ (care) mistake yesterday when he forgot to check a river for alligators before going swimming. Kaleb Langdale found himself in the [2] _____ (comfort) position of sharing the water with an alligator, which started to attack him. He was [3] _____ (luck) enough to escape the first attack and he began to swim to the bank, where his friends were [4] _____ (desperation) waiting for him. [5] _____ (fortune), the ten-foot animal attacked again, and this time it held on to Kaleb's arm. [6] _____ (luck), Kaleb managed to get away, but he lost his right arm in the process. Kaleb is now resting [7] _____ (comfort) in the hospital, despite his horrific injuries. He recommends that anybody who goes swimming in the Caloosahatchee River in Florida check the water [8] _____ (care) before jumping in.

4 LISTENING

a **ONLINE** Listen to five speakers talking about superstitions. Match the speakers with the pictures.

b Listen again and match the speakers with the sentences below.

Speaker 1 Speaker 4
 _b_   ___

Speaker 2 Speaker 5
 ___   ___

Speaker 3
 ___

a He / She was frustrated by this superstition.
b ~~He / She does something dangerous because of a superstition.~~
c He / She says that this superstition used to be a kind of self-defense.
d He / She does something to make something good happen.
e He / She says this superstition is associated with death.

c Listen again with the audioscript on p. 75.

5 READING

a Read the article once and number the paragraphs in the correct order.

A lucky escape

A ___ After he had seen the pictures of the crash, Mr. Hamilton called emergency services. The police came immediately and an ambulance arrived on the scene soon after. A spokesperson from the ambulance service said that the couple both had minor injuries, but only one of them had been taken to the hospital. A neighbor said that she had seen the young couple having an argument in the car when the accident happened.

B ___ Instead of going downstairs to talk to the couple in his yard, Mr. Hamilton went to look at the pictures on his security cameras. He had installed the cameras a few years earlier to deter people from stealing the potted plants outside his front door. The Hamiltons live on the corner of a road that leads to the main road, and passersby can easily step over the low wall that surrounds his yard. When he played back the pictures of the accident, he could not believe his eyes.

C _1_ An elderly couple from Central England, had a shock last night after they had gone to bed. Seventy-five-year old Howard Hamilton and his wife were just falling asleep when they heard a big bang in their front yard. They both jumped straight out of bed to look out the window and see what had happened. What they saw was a badly damaged car lying in their front yard. Next to the car there was a young couple hugging each other. Once Mr. Hamilton realized that nobody had been hurt, he decided to go and find out what had caused the accident.

D ___ Apparently, this is the fourth time that a car has driven through the wall of Mr. Hamilton's yard. This is because drivers often go around the corner too fast, and lose control of their vehicles. Mr. Hamilton's sister Joyce, who lives next door, said that it had been lucky that nobody had been walking on the sidewalk. She said that she didn't know what would have happened if there had been somebody there. Regarding the number of accidents that have happened on the corner, she said, "We're getting used to it."

E ___ On the recording, he saw that the girlfriend had been driving the car. He watched her turn the corner and lose control of the car. The car crashed right through the wall of his yard and came to a stop in the middle of the lawn. But the most dramatic thing is what had happened to her boyfriend. Before the crash, the sunroof of the car had been open. When the car hit the wall, Mr. Hamilton saw the boyfriend fly out of the sunroof and land heavily on the lawn. Miraculously, he was not hurt. Instead, he got up, and went to find his girlfriend. She didn't seem to be badly injured either – she appeared to be wearing her seat belt when the accident happened.

b Read the article in the correct order and answer the questions.

1. When did Mr. and Mrs. Hamilton hear the accident happen?
   They heard it after they had gone to bed.
2. What did they see when they looked out their bedroom window?
   _____
3. Why had Mr. Hamilton installed security cameras in his yard?
   _____
4. Why did the car crash through the wall of Mr. Hamilton's yard?
   _____
5. What happened to the boyfriend?
   _____
6. What happened to the couple when emergency services arrived?
   _____
7. What did a neighbor say about the couple in the accident?
   _____
8. Why are there so many accidents on that corner?
   _____

c Look at the highlighted words and phrases. What do you think they mean? Use your dictionary to look up their meaning and pronunciation.

d Complete the sentences with one of the highlighted words or phrases.

1. I _had a shock_ last night when the phone rang at midnight.
2. You should always call _____ _____ if there is a fire in your house.
3. The library is just _____ _____ _____ from my house.
4. Rachel fell off her bike yesterday, but luckily she only had _____ _____.
5. If you drive fast, it's easy to _____ _____ of the car and crash.
6. _____ described what happened to the police.

USEFUL WORDS AND PHRASES

Learn these words and phrases.

countryside /ˈkʌntrisaɪd/
stranger (noun) /ˈstreɪndʒər/
hitchhike /ˈhɪtʃhaɪk/
miss (the connection) /mɪs/
pour (gas into a car) /pɔr/
shiver /ˈʃɪvər/

upset (adj) /ʌpˈsɛt/
feel lonely /fil ˈloʊnli/
get to the (top) /ˈgɛt tə ðə/
in order to (do something) /ɪn ˈɔrdər tər/

> Computers are useless. They only give you answers.
> *Pablo Picasso, Spanish artist*

9B Too much information!

1 GRAMMAR quantifiers

a Circle the correct form.

1 *A lot of* / *A lot* people send text messages on the train.
2 There wasn't *no* / *any* bread left in the store by the time I got there.
3 Most of my friends spend *too many* / *too much* time on social networking sites.
4 This bag isn't *enough big* / *big enough* to put all my books in.
5 I like my coffee with just *a little* / *a few* hot milk.
6 I think people eat *too quickly* / *too much quickly* these days.
7 There were *lot* / *lots of* people waiting at the bus stop.
8 There's *no* / *any* time to stop for lunch. We'll just have to have a sandwich.
9 There were *very little* / *very few* tickets left for the concert.
10 There aren't *enough hours* / *hours enough* in the day to do everything.

b Complete each pair of sentences so that they have the same meaning. Sometimes more than one expression is possible.

1 There __aren't enough__ chairs.
  There are __too few__ chairs.

4 He has _____ video games.
  There aren't _____ shelves.

2 He can't afford it. He doesn't have _____ money.
  He can't afford it. It's _____ for him.

5 There's _____ gas in the tank.
  There isn't _____ gas in the tank.

3 We only had _____ sleep last night.
  We didn't have _____ sleep last night.

6 She buys very _____ books these days.
  She doesn't buy _____ books these days.

2 PRONUNCIATION -ough and -augh

a Circle the word with a different sound.

1 saw	2 up	3 saw	4 saw
(although)	cough	bought	caught
brought	enough	daughter	laughed
thought	tough	through	taught

b **ONLINE** Listen and check. Then listen again and repeat the words.

3 VOCABULARY phrasal verbs

a Complete the sentences with the simple past form of the phrasal verbs in the box. Replace the words in **bold** with a pronoun.

plug in ~~switch on~~ turn up turn down switch off

1 I wanted to listen **to the radio** so
    I _switched it on_.
2 **The music** was too loud so
    I _____.
3 When I found **my adaptor**,
    I _____.
4 I couldn't hear **my MP3 player** so
    I _____.
5 There wasn't anything on **TV** so
    I _____.

electronic devices

b Complete the crossword.

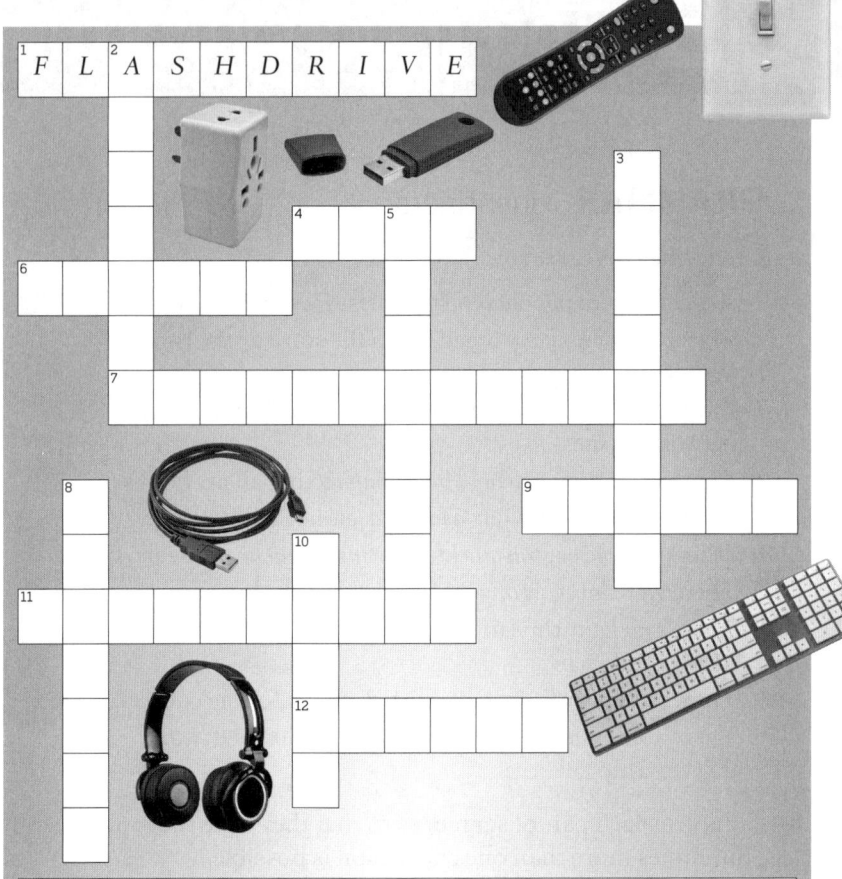

1 across: F L A S H D R I V E

Clues across →
1 A small device that can be used to store data and to move it from one computer to another.
4 A plastic object with two or three metal pins that connects electrical equipment to the electricity supply.
6 The place on a wall where electrical equipment can be connected to the electricity supply.
7 A piece of equipment for controlling something from a distance.
9 The lighted surface of a computer where the information appears.
11 A piece of equipment worn over the ears that makes it possible to listen to music without other people hearing it.
12 A small button that you press up and down in order to turn on electricity.

Clues down ↓
2 A device for connecting pieces of electrical equipment that were not designed to be fitted together.
3 The set of keys on a computer.
5 The piece of equipment for connecting other pieces of equipment to a computer.
8 A part of an electrical device that the sound comes out of.
10 A piece of equipment connected to a computer for moving around the screen and entering commands without touching the keys.

60

4 READING

a Read the article once and choose the best heading.

1. Laptops and modern lifestyles ☐
2. Eat and drink while you work ☐
3. Liquid and laptops don't mix ☐

Have you ever dropped a drink on your laptop? If you have, you'll remember the panic when you thought that your machine would never work again. If you haven't, it may well happen to you in the future. Spilling drinks on a laptop is a common occurrence. Just in case it does happen, here are some basic tips that tell you what you should do.

The effect of the drink on your laptop depends on what it is. Water and green tea generally cause the least damage. The worst drinks to spill are those that contain milk and sugar, such as hot drinks like coffee and tea, and soft drinks like soda or lemonade.

What happens to your laptop also depends on what you do immediately after the spill. The first thing you should do is unplug the machine and take the battery out. This will hopefully stop any electrical damage. Then, you should turn it upside down and stop the liquid from getting to the motherboard. This is where some of the most important parts of the computer are, and if it gets wet, your laptop may be damaged permanently.

The next step is to clean up as much of the liquid as quickly as possible. If you don't have a cloth to do this, use some tissues instead. Try to touch the keyboard lightly instead of wiping it with the tissue.

If you spilled a lot of liquid, you'll have to work harder to save your machine. Put it near a window or somewhere with cold air, and shake it gently to get the liquid out. It might help if you take off the bottom of the case so that you can take out the hard drive. If you do this, remember not to touch any of the electronics. When you have done as much as you can, leave the laptop somewhere warm to dry. This will take at least a day. Do not use a hair dryer because this will make the machine dirty.

When you think the laptop is dry, turn it back on to see if it works. If you only spilled a little clean water, you might be lucky and the machine may turn on right away. However, you'll probably have problems if the drink was a large, milky coffee with lots of sugar in it. If your laptop still doesn't work, look at the keyboard and try taking it apart to clean it better. However, if you've gone this far, it's probably time to think about getting some help. You can either take the laptop to be repaired, or buy a new one. And in the future, remember to drink your coffee at someone else's desk!

b Read the article again. Mark the sentences T (true) or F (false).

1. Not many people spill drinks on their laptops. _F_
2. Green tea causes less damage than coffee with milk. __
3. You shouldn't move your laptop after a spill. __
4. You should only use a cloth. __
5. You can try taking out the hard drive of the machine. __
6. You should use a hair dryer to dry the electronics. __
7. A little water doesn't usually cause much damage. __
8. The advice in the article only works for laptops that haven't had a lot of liquid spilled on them. __

c Look at the highlighted words and phrases. What do you think they mean? Use your dictionary to look up their meaning and pronunciation.

5 LISTENING

a ONLINE Listen to a conversation at the reception desk of a hotel. What does the guest want to know?

_____

b Listen again and complete the notes.

Name	¹ _Barry Gray_	Type of Wi-Fi chosen ⁶ _____
Room Number	² _____	Start time ⁷ _____
Standard	³ _____ per day	
Advanced	⁴ _____ per minute	End time ⁸ _____
Maximum	⁵ _____ per day	

c Listen again with the audioscript on p. 76.

USEFUL WORDS AND PHRASES

Learn these words and phrases.

hits (on a website) /hɪts/
willpower /ˈwɪlpaʊər/
multitask /ˈmʌltitæsk/
relevant /ˈrɛləvənt/
be productive /bi prəˈdʌktɪv/
feel anxious /fil ˈæŋkʃəs/
common sense /kɑmən ˈsɛns/
electronic device /ɪlɛkˈtrɑnɪk dɪˈvaɪs/
from time to time /frəm taɪm tə ˈtaɪm/
information overload /ɪnfərˈmeɪʃn oʊvərˈloʊd/

ONLINE **FILE 9**

Practical English Unexpected events

1 INDIRECT QUESTIONS

Correct any mistakes in the highlighted phrases. Check (✓) the correct sentences.

Ticket agent	Can I help you?
Max	Yes. I'd like to know what time is the next bus to Boston .

¹ _what time the next bus to Boston is_

Ticket agent	Well, the next bus leaves at 10 a.m.
Max	Great. Could you tell me how much costs a one-way ticket?

² _____

Ticket agent	Sure. A one-way ticket to Boston costs $35.95. Can you tell me do you have a Student Advantage Card ?

³ _____

Max	Yes, here it is.
Ticket agent	Then you get a 20% discount on your ticket. That means it'll cost you $28.75.
Max	Great! Here's my credit card.
Ticket agent	OK. And here's your ticket and your cards.
Max	Thanks. Can you tell me if I need to change buses ?

⁴ _____

Ticket agent	No, you don't. The bus goes straight through.
Max	And do you know what time does it arrive ?

⁵ _____

Ticket agent	Yes, it gets in at 2:20 p.m.
Max	Thanks a lot.

2 SOCIAL ENGLISH

Complete the dialogue with the words and phrases in the box.

| either | I guess | It's obvious | Of course | ~~Stop it!~~ | What if |

A ¹ _Stop it!_ You keep yawning. Everyone will think you're bored.
B Oh, sorry. ² _____ I'm a little tired.
A ³ _____ you're tired. You had a long day.
B Well, I did get up at six o'clock this morning.
A Oh, come on. Let's go. ⁴ _____ you aren't enjoying the party.
B I'm sorry. I think I need to go to bed.
A I know. ⁵ _____ we go home and do something fun tomorrow?
B That sounds like a great idea. And I promise I won't yawn all day, ⁶ _____ .
A Perfect!

3 READING

a Read the text. Mark the sentences T (true) or F (false).

1 People made bread in the shape of bagels in many different cultures. _T_
2 Bagels were first made in Austria. ___
3 They were made by Jewish bakers. ___
4 Bagels first came to the US in 1900. ___
5 They became popular all over America in the 1960s. ___
6 New inventions were used to sell bagels across America. ___
7 One of the reasons bagels are popular is because they stay fresh longer than bread. ___

A Short History of the Bagel

The bagel is known around the world as a typically New York type of food. But it has a surprising and unusual history that goes back many years.

The basic idea of a bread roll with a hole is centuries old. In Roman times, soldiers ate hard bread called *buccellatum*, and in China there is similar-shaped traditional bread called *girde*. The ancient Egyptians ate a bagel-like snack, too, and there are even more examples from around the Mediterranean area.

But it was in Poland that today's bagel really began. According to legend, it was the product of the 1683 Battle of Vienna. The Polish king, Jan Sobieski, had saved Austria from the Turkish invaders. To celebrate, the Jewish bakers of Kraków made a roll in the shape of the king's stirrup – the metal objects you put your feet in when you ride a horse – and called it a "buegel" (from the German word for stirrup). There is, however, no evidence to show whether this was true or not, but the story still remains today.

It is unclear when the first bagels made their way to the United States, but by 1900, there were 70 bakeries that sold bagels on the Lower East Side of New York. What is also certain is that immigrants from Eastern Europe, with their cravings for the foods of the old country, sparked the New York bagel craze.

It was the 1950s that were the real turning point. As Jewish people began to move to other parts of New York, they started to share their traditional food with the rest of the city. Bagels were mentioned in a popular cookbook of the time, and demand started to grow across America. To meet this demand, a baker named Murray Lender began to use recent inventions like the freezer and plastic packaging to distribute freshly made bagels across America. Soon, Lender's bagels were available in almost every supermarket, and today they are part of a typical American diet and available all over the world.

But why has the bagel endured through all this time? Possibly because of its heroic legend, but also because it has the advantage of lasting longer than freshly baked bread. If it gets slightly stale, it can be dunked in hot liquid to soften it. So it lasts long, can be eaten in many ways, and of course tastes delicious.

b Underline five words or phrases you don't know. Use your dictionary to look up their meaning and pronunciation.

> I don't think that I want to meet any of the icons. I don't think that anybody can quite live up to your expectations.
>
> Jane Horrocks, English actress

10A Modern icons

1 GRAMMAR relative clauses: defining and non-defining

a Complete the sentences with a relative pronoun. Where two answers are possible, write both pronouns. There is one sentence where you can leave out the relative pronoun.

1. Espoo is the city in Finland __where__ Nokia is based.
2. Apple is the company __which / that__ makes the iPad.
3. Melinda Gates is the woman _____ husband founded Microsoft.
4. The thing _____ my son wants most for his birthday is a tablet computer.
5. Lee Byung-chull was the man _____ founded Samsung.
6. Minato, is the district in Tokyo _____ Sony has its headquarters.
7. Alexander Graham Bell is the man _____ invented the telephone.

b Cross out the extra word in each of the sentences.

1. Why don't you stay in the hotel where we stayed ~~there~~ last year?
2. He's the actor who he played the role of Sherlock Holmes.
3. Those are the students who they won first prize.
4. I'll go to the supermarket that it has the best offers.
5. She's the woman whose her daughter went to the same school as me.
6. What's the name of the store where we bought the USB cable there?
7. That's the computer that it isn't working.

c Complete the sentences with a relative pronoun and the phrases in the box. You will need to leave out one of the words in each of the phrases.

~~he has appeared in several James Bond movies~~	she is a human rights leader
her voice will never be forgotten	it is in the Andes
his wife is the singer Beyoncé	the Mona Lisa can be seen there
Native Americans protected themselves from hot temperatures there	it was opened in China in 2011

1. Daniel Craig, __who has appeared in several James Bond movies__, was born in Chester.

2. The Louvre, _____ _____, is in the center of Paris.

3. Aconcagua, _____ _____, is the highest mountain in South America.

4. Selena, _____ _____, died in 1995.

5. Jiaozhou Bay Bridge, _____ _____, is the longest bridge in the world.

6. Aung San Suu Kyi, _____ _____, was under house arrest for 15 years.

7. Jay-Z, _____ _____, is one of the most successful rappers of all time.

8. The Cliff Palace, _____ _____, is in the US.

2 VOCABULARY compound nouns

a Write the compound noun for each picture.

 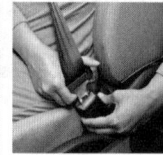  

1 _website_   2 s_____   3 h_____   4 pr_____
              b_____   p_____

5 tr_____   6 f_____   7 b_____   8 s_____
  j_____   fl_____   m_____

b Match a word from A with a word from B to make compound nouns. Then complete the sentences.

A	~~bank~~ high bicycle room rush sound top training
B	~~account~~ course floor hour lane mate school track

1 My salary is deposited directly into my _bank account_ every month.
2 They live on the _____ _____, so they have a great view of the city.
3 The _____ for the movie *The Hobbit* is awesome.
4 My brother is taking a _____ _____ to learn about health and safety.
5 Do you get along well with your _____ or do you argue about paying the bills?
6 The first year of _____ _____ in the US is usually ninth grade.
7 Bike riders should use the _____ _____ to keep away from traffic.
8 Commuters usually travel to work during _____ _____.

3 PRONUNCIATION word stress

a Match the words 1–8 with the words in the box to make compound nouns.

| cam|era   court   drive   map   ~~pass~~ |
| ti|cket   tone   walk |

1 boar|ding _pass_   5 ring_____
2 cross_____   6 speed_____
3 flash_____   7 sub|way_____
4 par|king_____   8 te|nnis_____

b ONLINE Listen and check. Then listen again and repeat the words. <u>Un</u>derline the stressed syllables.

4 READING

a Read some extracts from an interview with Usain Bolt once. What do you learn about his family?
1 He has _____.
2 He lives with _____.

Children, adults, old people… everybody wants to race me. I get challenged to races every day. I met Mickey Rourke in a dance club and we had a race in the street. I'll race the kids, but grown-up people need to get real.

I am an athlete and a doctor. I have received lots of honorary degrees, so my full official title is something like Dr. The Honorable Ambassador Usain Saint Leo Bolt. I have tried to make my friends call me it, but nobody does.

My father was my hero. He always worked so hard. People think I don't train hard, but I really do – and it's all because of him.

My earliest memory is playing in my yard. I'd play cricket, soccer, and basketball or just run around. As long as I was outside in the sun I was happy.

Your environment definitely changes your personality. I am similar to my sister. We are relaxed because we grew up in the country (in Jamaica), but my brother is different because he grew up in Kingston.

Sleep is beautiful. I live with my brother Sadiki and my best friend NJ in Kingston, and my only house rule is: never wake me up early.

I can't cook. I just know that vegetables are good for you.

What I enjoy most about my house isn't the big TV or the swimming pool, but the fruit trees in my yard. They remind me of my childhood. When I sit and stare at them I feel happy. I like to sit under trees.

Snakes and spiders terrify me. That's why I don't go to Africa very often. I also used to believe in ghosts when I was a kid and I would get scared, but not anymore.

Bob Marley is a legend. I have all his old albums, and he did a great job of bringing Jamaica to the world.

I can be emotional. I cried at a movie last year – but don't tell anyone.

I have always been young and fast…so the idea of being old feels weird. I do worry about it. My friend NJ is a couple of months older than me, so I will always be younger than him. That makes me feel better.

b Read the interview again and answer the questions.

1. Who doesn't Usain Bolt mind racing?
   Children.
2. Which member of his family does he admire the most?
3. What did he enjoy doing when he was a child?
4. What doesn't he like doing?
5. What isn't he very good at?
6. What does he like most about his house?
7. What is he afraid of?
8. Which singer does he like?
9. What happened when he went to the movies last year?
10. What does he worry about?

c Look at the highlighted words and phrases. What do you think they mean? Use your dictionary to look up their meaning and pronunciation.

d Complete the sentences with the highlighted words.

1. We have a _house_ _rule_ that the person who cooks doesn't have to wash the dishes.
2. My car is making a _____ noise – I have no idea what it is, but it doesn't sound good.
3. I told my sister to _____ _____ – she'll never have a big house on the beach.
4. Miles Davis is a _____ of jazz music.
5. American colleges often give _____ _____ to celebrities who didn't study there, but who have done work for charities or have inspired students.

5 LISTENING

a ONLINE Listen to a radio program about a new exhibition at the Science Museum. Check (✓) the two inventions mentioned in the program and label the two pictures you check.

1 _____ 2 _____ 3 _____

4 _____ 5 _____ 6 _____

b Listen again and mark the sentences T (true) or F (false).

1. The exhibition shows very special things that we don't often use. _F_
2. Napoleon Bonaparte had a problem feeding all his soldiers. ___
3. A French soldier won the competition. ___
4. The first design was made of metal. ___
5. A later design killed a number of people. ___
6. In the past, people bought a big box of leaves to make tea with. ___
7. Thomas Sullivan sold the small bags of tea to his customers. ___
8. He told his customers not to open the tea bags. ___
9. Tea bags were really invented by some of his customers. ___
10. The exhibition closes on Sunday, July 25th. ___

c Listen again with the audioscript on p. 76.

USEFUL WORDS AND PHRASES

Learn these words and phrases.

icon /ˈaɪkɑn/
logo /ˈloʊgoʊ/
silhouette /ˌsɪluˈɛt/
incorporate /ɪnˈkɔrpəreɪt/
manufacture /ˌmænyəˈfæktʃər/
be adopted /bi əˈdɑptəd/
drop out (from school) /drɑp ˈaʊt/
found a company /faʊnd ə ˈkʌmpəni/
a worldwide (Internet) sensation /ə ˌwɜrldˈwaɪd sɛnˈseɪʃn/

> Poetry is not the most important thing in life. I'd much rather lie in a hot bath reading Agatha Christie and sucking sweets.
>
> Dylan Thomas, Welsh poet

10B Two crime stories

1 VOCABULARY crime

Complete the text.

¹ D<u>etectives</u> are investigating a ² m_____ in Millbrook. The ³ v_____ is a 26-year-old man whose body was found last night next to a quiet, back road. No ⁴ ev_____ was found at the scene and police are appealing to ⁵ w_____ who saw the man yesterday to help them with their investigation. They believe that the ⁶ m_____ was someone known to the man. The main ⁷ s_____ are the man's roommate, his girlfriend, and a neighbor. These people are currently being interviewed by the police in an attempt to ⁸ s_____ the crime. A police spokesperson said that they had a theory, but so far, they had been unable to ⁹ pr_____ who had committed the crime.

2 GRAMMAR tag questions

a Circle the correct answers.
1 You live in Seattle, *don't you* / aren't you?
2 But you weren't born in Seattle, weren't you / were you?
3 You moved to Seattle when you were ten, weren't you / didn't you?
4 That means you've been living here for twenty years, haven't you / have you?
5 But you're moving to Los Angeles next week, won't you / aren't you?
6 Your brother lives in Los Angeles, doesn't he / isn't he?
7 You've been in prison before, aren't you / haven't you?
8 I guess you'd like to call your lawyer now, don't you / wouldn't you?

b Complete the tag questions.
1 Adam's living with his parents now, _isn't he_?
2 You don't like animals, _____?
3 It isn't difficult, _____?
4 He drives a van, _____?
5 They left yesterday, _____?
6 Kathy hasn't been home for over a week, _____?
7 I'm late, _____?
8 You'll see him tomorrow, _____?

3 PRONUNCIATION intonation in tag questions

a **ONLINE** Listen and repeat the sentences. Copy the rhythm.
1 You **called** her **last night**, **didn't you**?
2 He's **older** than **you**, **isn't he**?
3 They **aren't coming**, **are they**?
4 You'd **like** to **visit Paris**, **wouldn't you**?
5 She'll be **late**, **won't she**?
6 I **can't dance** very **well**, **can I**?

b Write the words in the box in the correct columns.

brutal suspect hurt ~~murder~~ prove truth discover suddenly we**re**n't

1 ɜr bird	2 u boot	3 ʌ up
murder		

c **ONLINE** Listen and check. Then listen again and repeat the words.

4 READING

a Read part 1 of an extract from a novel once. Where does Hannay first think Scudder is from?

England ☐
Norway ☐
the US ☐
Greece ☐

The Thirty-Nine Steps

Introduction:
Richard Hannay, the narrator, has just returned to London from Africa. A mysterious man called Franklin Scudder appears outside his flat one night, and tells Hannay about a group of people he met who are trying to push Europe towards a war. He believes only the Greek Prime Minister, Constantine Karolides, can stop the war. Karolides will be in London soon, and Scudder believes there is a plan to kill him then. Scudder believes he can stop this plan, but only if people think he is dead…

Part 1
I was beginning to like this strange little man. I gave him another drink and asked him why he thought he was now in danger himself.

He took a large mouthful. "I came to London by a strange route – through Paris, Hamburg, Norway, and Scotland. I changed my name in every country, and when I got to London, I thought I was safe. There's a man watching this building and last night somebody put a card under my door. On it was the name of the man I fear most in the world.

"So I decided I had to 'die.' Then they would stop looking for me. I got a dead body – it's easy to get one in London, if you know how – and I had the body brought to my flat in a large suitcase. The body was the right age, but the face was different from mine. I dressed it in my clothes and shot it in the face with my own gun. My servant will find me when he arrives in the morning and he'll call the police. I've left a lot of empty bottles in my room. The police will think I drank too much and then killed myself." He paused. "I watched from the window until I saw you come home, and then came down the stairs to meet you."

It was the strangest of stories. However, in my experience, the most extraordinary stories are often the true ones. And if the man just wanted to get into my flat and murder me, why didn't he tell a simpler story? "Right," I said. "I'll trust you for tonight. I'll lock you in this room and keep the key. Just one word, Mr. Scudder. I believe you're honest, but if you're not, I should warn you that I certainly know how to use a gun."

"Certainly," he answered, jumping up. "I'm afraid I don't know your name, sir, but I would like to thank you. And could I use your bathroom?"

When I saw him next, half an hour later, I didn't recognize him at first. Only the bright eyes were the same. His beard was gone, and his hair was completely different. He walked like a soldier, and he was wearing glasses. And he no longer spoke like an American.

"Mr. Scudder – " I cried.

"Not Mr. Scudder," he answered. "Captain Theophilus Digby of the British Army. Please do remember that."

I made him a bed in my study, and went to bed myself, happier than I had been for the past month. Interesting things did happen sometimes, even in London.

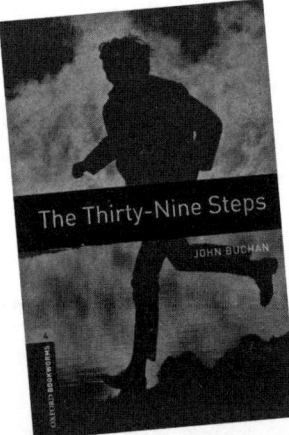

Extract from Oxford Bookworms Library:
The Thirty-Nine Steps by John Buchanan, retold by Nick Bullard
© Oxford University Press 2007.

b Read the extract again and choose the best answers.

1 The man took a strange route to London because…
   a he wanted to see all the sights.
   b he got lost on the way.
   c he didn't want anybody to find him.
2 The person who sent him a card last night is…
   a a friend.
   b an enemy.
   c a colleague.
3 The man is pretending to be dead because…
   a he wants people to stop looking for him.
   b he owes someone a lot of money.
   c he doesn't want to talk to the police.
4 The narrator, Hannay, trusts the man because…
   a he knows him very well.
   b his story is so complicated.
   c he doesn't look like a murderer.
5 When the man went to the bathroom, he…
   a took a bath.
   b combed his hair.
   c put on a disguise.
6 The man spent the night…
   a in Hannay's apartment.
   b in a hotel.
   c in his own apartment.
7 The man changes his name to a…
   a French name.
   b British name.
   c German name.
8 Hannay now thinks that…
   a nothing exciting happens in London.
   b it's always interesting in London.
   c something exciting can happen in London.

c Underline six words or phrases you don't know. Use your dictionary to look up their meaning and pronunciation.

5 LISTENING

a ONLINE Listen to Part 2 of the extract. What happens to Mr. Scudder?

b Listen again and mark the answers T (true) or F (false).

1 The narrator told his servant who Scudder really was the next morning. _F_
2 Mr. Scudder's plan to pretend to commit suicide worked. ___
3 Mr. Scudder was calm and relaxed all the time he was in Hannay's apartment. ___
4 He gave Hannay more details about the plot to kill Karolides. ___
5 Apart from Karolides, he mentioned one other person. ___
6 The study light was on when the narrator got home. ___

c Listen again with the audioscript on p. 76.

USEFUL WORDS AND PHRASES

Learn these words and phrases.

alibi /ˈæləbaɪ/
case /keɪs/
court /kɔrt/
the defense /ðə dɪˈfɛns/
the dock (of a court) /ðə dɑk/
the prosecution /ðə prɑsəˈkyuʃn/
trial /ˈtraɪəl/
plead (guilty / innocent) /plid/
swear (e.g., on the bible) /swɛr/
be acquitted /bi əˈkwɪtəd/

ONLINE FILE 10

Listening

1 A)

Host Welcome back to the show. Today, we've been discussing Teresa Gold's article *The Truth About Healthy Eating*. And now it's time for you, the listeners, to tell us what you think. The lines are open, so all you have to do is call 1-800-555-5792 and talk to one of our operators. That's 1-800-555-5792. And it looks like we have our first caller. Kevin from Miami, tell us what you think about the article.

Kevin Well, I'd like to say that I don't agree with the article at all. I don't eat many fruits or vegetables, and I'm perfectly healthy. I haven't called in sick to work for years – I can't remember the last time I had to stay in bed. This five-a-day thing is garbage, isn't it?

Host Um … thank you, Kevin. I think we have another caller on line two. Kate from Chicago, are you there?

Kate Yes, I am. Well, I'm sure the writer knows what she's talking about, but it isn't that easy. I mean, it's hard enough to get kids to eat vegetables at the best of times, but with all these burger and pizza places around, it's almost impossible. Once they get the taste for junk food, you can forget the five-a-day, that's for sure!

Host Thanks, Kate. And who's our next caller?

Derek Um, my name's Derek and I'm from Washington, D.C.

Host And what do you think, Derek?

Derek Well, I'd like to say that I think that the article is right. I mean, the writer talks about eating a lot of fruits and vegetables, which is something that we've always done in my family. My mom's a great cook. She always uses completely natural ingredients in her cooking, and we're almost never sick….

Host Thank you, Derek. Let's go back to line two again, where we have Rosie from Boston. Rosie, what's your opinion?

Rosie Well, the writer seems to think that ALL fruits and vegetables are good for you, and I don't think that's true. I mean, what about potatoes? They contain a lot of carbohydrates, which can make you gain weight if you aren't careful – it's even worse if you fry them. And then some fruits, like melon for example, have a lot of sugar. Personally, I think you should eat a little of everything and not too much of one thing.

Host Thanks, Rosie. And that's all the time we have for today. We'll be speaking to the writer of the article after the break.

1 B)

Terry I'm exhausted!
Jane Me too. I haven't stopped all day.
Terry Neither have I.
Jane Oh, well. I guess it'll get easier when the kids grow up.
Terry Do you think so?
Jane Of course. When they're older, they'll be more independent. We won't have to do everything for them anymore.
Terry And how long will that take? Five, six years? Or maybe never!
Jane Look, what's the problem, Terry?
Terry Nothing. It's just that we never have time for each other these days. We're always with the kids!
Jane But that's what happens when you have kids. It'll get better!
Terry I don't know… My parents were talking about us going to live with them. Do you think it would be easier for us if we lived with my parents?
Jane Well, I guess it'd have its advantages.
Terry Yeah, I mean for one thing there'd always be someone to take care of the kids.
Jane That sounds good.
Terry And we could go out in the evening without the kids. Just imagine that!
Jane Hmm. That doesn't really matter to me.
Terry And there would be more people to share the housework, too. It wouldn't always be the same person who does the shopping, cleans the house, and cooks the meals.
Jane Yes, but there would be more people in the house, so there would be more work to do. Shopping and cooking for six isn't the same as doing it for four.
Terry I guess so.
Jane And another disadvantage is that we wouldn't have any privacy.
Terry True.
Jane And you know what your parents are like. They let the kids do everything they want to do.
Terry Hmm. I guess you don't want to move in with my parents, then.
Jane Not really, no. Would you like to move in with mine?
Terry No, definitely not … Actually, things aren't so bad right now.
Jane I agree.
Terry And the kids will be older soon.
Jane Yes, they will.
Terry That's settled then. We're staying here.
Jane Fine.

2 A)

Speaker 1: Can I live on my salary? Well, I don't really have many problems, because I'm still living with my mom and dad. Don't get me wrong, I give my mom some money for rent, but it's definitely much cheaper than living on your own. I actually have a pretty good salary – I'm a graphic designer. I don't really spend much – I buy some new clothes every now and then, and I have to put gas in my car, of course, but apart from that, it's really just going out on the weekends. Most of my money goes into a savings account so that I can buy my own house one day.

Speaker 2: I find it really hard to live on my income because I only have a part-time job. Being on my own with my daughter means that my mom has to take care of her when I'm at work. At least I don't have to pay for childcare! The house we live in is rented, so that's where most of the money goes. I don't think I'll ever be able to afford our own place because the bank won't give me a mortgage. Apart from the rent, my money goes to food and clothes for my daughter. Still, I shouldn't complain. I have an amazing daughter, and that's all that really matters.

Speaker 3: I think I'm really lucky. I'm pretty healthy for my age, I have enough money to live on, and I have my children and grandchildren! When I say I have enough money, I don't go on any fancy vacations or anything like that. But I'm comfortable. I've paid the mortgage, so that's one less expense, and I don't have any loans to pay either. My one little luxury is going out for lunch a few times a week with some friends. I guess that's where most of my money goes – on food!

Speaker 4: Can we live on our salaries? Well, I'm not so sure, actually! My husband is a teacher, so he doesn't earn that much – definitely not enough to raise two children! That means I have to work, too – I have a full-time job at the local supermarket. And really, that's our biggest problem, because we need someone to take care of the children. Our babysitter costs a fortune – we spend more on child care than we do on our mortgage! Then there's food and new clothes for the children, too. Honestly, it isn't cheap having kids these days!

2 B))

Host And now to end the show with an inspirational story, we have John to tell us about an incredible trip.

John Yes, thank you, Nora. Have you ever thought about traveling around the world and trying to help people as you go? Well that's what an American father and his two adopted sons are currently doing. J.D. Lewis is a single parent and a former actor. He's taken his sons, Jackson, age 14 and Buck, age 9, out of school for a year to make the trip with him. And their plan is to help people along the way by doing volunteer charity work.

Host That sounds wonderful, but it must be an expensive trip. How much will it all cost?

John It's going to cost them $300,000 dollars in total.

Host That's a lot of money. How did they afford it?

John Well, J.D Lewis didn't have all the money, so he set up an organization called Twelve in Twelve to help raise money, and with the help of individuals and some companies, they managed to raise the money.

Host Twelve in Twelve – that's an unusual name. Why did he call it that?

John For a very good reason. Not only is their trip going to last twelve months, but their plan is to visit twelve countries. This month, they're in Australia, where they're working with the most important ethnic group in the region – the Aborigines. J.D and his family are helping to get medical supplies to these people, who often live a long way from the major cities.

Host And is that the first place they've visited?

John Oh, no. So far they've visited seven countries. Their first stop was Russia, where they took care of babies in an orphanage in the city of Tomsk. From there, they traveled to China, where they worked with children with physical disabilities in Beijing. Then, they flew to Thailand where they helped take care of the animals at the Elephant Nature Park.

Host What a variety of places. Where did they go next?

John Their next stop was India, where they worked with children in the poorest district of the city of Hubli. Then they left Asia and flew to Africa. In Rwanda, they taught English to children who had lost their parents in the civil war. From there, they went to Zanzibar, an island off the coast of Tanzania.

Host That sounds very exotic! What did they do there?

John They helped families prepare an art fair, where they could sell things that they had made. Next, they went to Kenya, where they wrote and acted in a play with children who have HIV.

Host Wow, I bet that was very rewarding. Did they go anywhere else in Africa?

John No, that was the end of Africa. From Kenya, they flew to Australia, which is where they are right now.

Host All that sounds amazing, but their trip isn't over, is it?

John No, J.D. and his family still have four places to go: Antarctica, Paraguay, Peru, and Haiti. Not only are they trying to do things to help other people, but they are hoping to learn a lot of new things themselves. And J.D. Lewis hopes that the Twelve in Twelve organization will encourage other families to do what he has done with his sons.

Host Well, good luck to J.D. Lewis and his family on the rest of their incredible trip. And that's all we have time for tonight. Join us again tomorrow when we'll be bringing you more real-life stories.

3 A))

Speaker 1: One morning last winter, I was driving to work late when my cell phone rang. I knew it was my boss, so I answered it. Suddenly, the van in front of me stopped because there was someone crossing the road. I was talking to my boss, so I reacted too late, and my car went into the back of the van. Luckily, I was driving really slowly at the time, so I didn't do much damage to the van, but the front of my car was a real mess. Since then, I never use my phone when I'm driving.

Speaker 2: I was driving to Colorado one summer to visit my parents, who live in Denver. It's a long trip, so I had taken my MP3 player with me to connect to the car radio. Surprisingly, there wasn't much traffic on the freeway, so I arrived in Denver pretty quickly. However, I was having such a good time listening to my music, that I completely missed the exits for Denver. I didn't realize until I had gone another 20 miles, so I had to turn around and drive all the way back again! It just goes to show what can happen when you aren't concentrating.

Speaker 3: We were on vacation last year, when we had a little accident. We were going somewhere we'd never been before, so we were following the instructions on my GPS. We heard on the radio that there'd been a big accident on one of the roads we needed to travel on, so I started adjusting my GPS to find a different road to take. I took my eyes off the road and suddenly we came to a sharp turn in the road. I saw the turn too late, so I went straight ahead and drove into the middle of a field. We were really lucky, though, because no one was hurt.

Speaker 4: I don't usually get up early enough to put my makeup on, so I usually put it on in my car. Well, I used to put it on in the car – now I wait until I get to my office. That's because I had kind of a shock the other week, when I almost didn't stop at a crosswalk. I was looking in the mirror instead of at the road, so I didn't see this little boy run out—to tell you the truth, I hadn't even seen that there was a crosswalk there. I just had time to step on the brakes and I missed the little boy by about an inch. I was really shocked afterward, though.

Speaker 5: I was driving into town to meet my girlfriend for dinner when she sent me a text message. I decided to read it, in case it was important. Anyway, the message said that my girlfriend was already at the restaurant, and I wanted her to know that I was going to be a little late, so when I stopped at a red light, I started to write a reply. But I didn't notice when the traffic light turned green, and the car behind crashed into the back of me. The driver of the car said he thought I was going to start driving, so he moved forward and hit me. Of course I didn't tell him I was texting.

3 B

Host Traditionally in the US, women have cooked more than men, but it looks as though things might be changing. According to a recent survey by a frozen foods company, almost half of all men in this country now prepare the family meals. And they aren't just doing it because they have to – it's because they enjoy it. The survey showed that 44 percent of men who were questioned do all of the cooking, and surprisingly, 15 percent of women questioned said that they didn't know *how* to cook. So it seems as if men are moving into the kitchen, and maybe women are moving out. Is this good news? What do you think? Call us at 1-800-555-3364 and tell us your opinion. I'll give you that number again – that's 1-800-555-3364.

And here's our first caller, Nick from San Diego, California. Nick, what do you think about this new trend?

Nick I'm pretty excited to see more men in the kitchen. In fact, I'm one of them! I lost my job a few months ago, and now I do all the cooking at home. I make a different dish every day, and sometimes I meet up with my friends to exchange recipes. My girlfriend says she really likes my food, and she even thinks that I should train to be a professional chef. I'm seriously thinking about doing that.

Host Well, good luck to you, Nick. Who's our next caller? Ah, yes … It's Eve from Seattle, Washington. Do you cook, Eve?

Eve No, I don't. But my husband does. He's a much better cook than I am, so we decided from the beginning that he would do all the cooking. And he makes some great meals – mostly curries. But there's one problem.

Host What's that, Eve?

Eve He makes a terrible mess in the kitchen, and I have to clean up after him. I don't know what's worse, actually, cooking myself or cleaning the kitchen!

Host Oh, come on Eve – it can't be that bad! Now I think we have someone on line 2. Yes, it's Frank from Hartford. What do you think about men taking over the kitchen, Frank?

Frank Well, I'm not surprised, to be honest with you. It seems to me that girls are getting lazier and lazier these days – it's only the older moms and grandmothers who know how to cook. I mean, how can a woman get married if she can't cook?! I think it's a disgrace!

Host Thank you, Frank. So, not all of our listeners think it's a good thing. How about our next caller, Martina, calling from South Florida? Is it good news or bad news for you, Martina?

Martina Good news. Definitely. In my house, I do all the cooking. My boyfriend doesn't cook at all – he can't even fry an egg! I mean, we both work full time, so why can't we share the cooking? I'm really fed up with it, I really am. But I'm really happy for all those women out there who have found a real man. I know how you feel when you have to do everything yourself.

Host Let's hope Martina's boyfriend is listening, so that he knows how she feels. We'll take some more calls after the break.

4 A

Speaker 1: I suffer from asthma and I usually carry an inhaler around with me just in case I get an attack. Anyway, I was on a work trip – I was in Paris – I had forgotten my inhaler, and I was having problems breathing. So I went to a pharmacy and asked for "un aspirateur," which I thought was the French word for inhaler. I realized it wasn't when the girls behind the counter looked very confused. It turned out that I had asked for a vacuum cleaner, "aspirateur," instead of an inhaler, "inhalateur."

Speaker 2: I was in Istanbul with a Turkish friend of mine, and we decided that we wanted to buy some bread. I wanted to try out the Turkish I knew, so I said that I would ask for it. So we found this tiny little store and we went in. I said to the salesperson in my best voice "taze erkek" which I thought meant "fresh bread." Unfortunately, I got the word for bread "ekmek" confused with the word for man "erkek," so what I had actually asked for was "a fresh young man." Luckily, my friend came to my rescue and asked for the bread correctly, but I felt a little embarrassed!

Speaker 3: I was 14, and I was on an exchange visit with my school in Madrid. It was the first night, and I was at home with my Spanish host family, the Garcías, having dinner. We'd finished the main course and it was time for dessert, so the wife, Maria, asked me if I'd like some fruit. I saw some bananas in the fruit bowl, so I asked for a "platón," at which point the whole family looked at me strangely. They then explained to me that I'd actually asked for a large plate. "Platón" means "large plate" whereas "banana" is "plátano."

Speaker 4: I was in Rio De Janeiro in Brazil with my husband, and it was a very hot day, so we decided to take a break from our sightseeing. We found a street vendor selling cold drinks and snacks near the beach. I was so hot and tired that I quickly ordered what I thought was ice cream. I said "uma cosquinha por favor." As soon as I'd finished speaking, the street vendor burst out laughing. He quickly apologized and explained in English that I'd asked him for a tickle and not ice cream. Tickle in Portuguese is "cosquinha" and ice cream is "casquinha."

Speaker 5: I'm an American living in Korea. Usually, I can communicate pretty well in Korean. I speak Korean with my wife every day, and I have a tutor that I meet with every week to practice my conversation skills. So, one day I went to the store to buy a few things. I usually take my young son with me, but he wasn't with me this particular day. When the salesperson asked me about my son, my answer confused her because I accidentally said "eh-jeh uhb-suh-yo," which means "he's dead." What I meant to say was "Yuh-gi uhb-suh-yo" which means "he's not here."

4 B

Host Hello and welcome to *The Traveler's Guide*. Now, last week we asked our listeners who are going to travel abroad to send us their questions about good manners in other countries, and we've invited our resident expert Ruth Dempsey to the show to answer them. Welcome to the program, Ruth.

Ruth Thank you.

Host So the first question, Ruth. This comes from Katy in Denver, who is going to travel around Thailand next summer. Katy wants to know what she should do when she first meets people in Thailand.

Ruth Well, Katy, most of the time, a simple handshake will be fine. But if someone gives you a "wai", that is a small bow with the hands held together close to the body, you must do the same. But, if the person is of lower social status than you, so if they are younger than you, or they are a waiter, for example, you shouldn't return the "wai."

Host Very useful advice, Ruth. The next question is from Mark in Dallas, who is going to Brazil with his girlfriend, to meet her family for the first time. He asks: "Is there anything I should or shouldn't do?"

Ruth Like Americans, Brazilians are very warm, friendly, and open. However, there are a few differences to remember. Always say thank you when someone opens a door for you, offers you something to eat or drink, or even when your girlfriend's mother clears the plates from the table. It's very important to be polite. Also, don't speak when you have food in your mouth. Brazilians find this incredibly rude.

Host That sounds like good advice for you, Mark. OK, our next question is from Julie in Oklahoma City. She's going to Greece on vacation, but doesn't speak the language. She asks: "Since I don't speak any Greek, I'll be communicating mostly with my hands. Are there any gestures I shouldn't use?"

Ruth Absolutely, Julie. The most important one to remember is the "thumbs up," which in the US means "good" or "OK." But it is very insulting to a Greek person. Another one is the US hand gesture for "stop," where you show someone your hand with your fingers straight together, like a police officer. But again this is an insult in Greece.

Host Good luck, Julie. And we have time for one more, and this question is from Kendra in Chicago. She's going to South Korea for work, and she would like some tips on business behavior over there.

Ruth The most important thing to remember is that South Koreans like to bow a lot. As a foreigner, you won't be expected to, but it is a good way of showing respect, and the deeper you bow, the happier you are.

Host Very interesting. Ruth Dempsey, thank you for joining us.

Ruth My pleasure.

Host And we'll be right back after a check of the headlines.

5 A))

Host Welcome back to the show. We've been talking about famous sports cheaters on today's program, and now we're going to hear about another scandal. The sport was badminton, and the venue was the 2012 Olympic Games in London. Tom is here to tell us about it. Hi, Tom.

Tom Hello, everybody.

Host So who was involved in the scandal, Tom?

Tom Well, the scandal involved four of the teams in the women's doubles competition. In total, eight players were disqualified for cheating: two pairs from South Korea, a pair from China, and a pair from Indonesia.

Host And what exactly happened?

Tom Well, basically the teams played badly on purpose to make sure they lost their matches.

Host Why would they do that?

Tom Well, to explain that I'll very quickly tell you about how the competition works. The matches are divided into different stages. Teams play against other teams in their group in the first stage, and if they win, they play in the next stage. So sometimes, a team might get a good opponent very early in the competition, which means it might not get through to the next stage.

Host Got it. So when did the cheating happen?

Tom Well, the problem started on the last day of the first stage. In the morning, the first Chinese team won its match, finishing second in its group. The second Chinese team was going to play against a South Korean team that evening, and whichever team won that match would most likely play against the first Chinese team in the next stage.

Host Why was this a problem?

Tom Neither team wanted to play against the first Chinese team because the South Korean team was sure it would lose, and the second Chinese team didn't want to play against a team from the same country yet, because that would mean that only one Chinese team was left to try to win a medal. So both teams tried to lose against each other instead.

Host How did they do that?

Tom Well, both the South Koreans and the second Chinese team started missing shots. When they served, they either hit the shuttlecock into the net or they hit it so hard that it went outside the lines on the court. In the end, they looked like amateurs, when in fact, they were some of the best players in the world.

Host So who lost the match?

Tom The second Chinese team. South Korea beat them in both sets.

Host What about the other two teams?

Tom Well, they tried to do exactly the same thing in the next match.

Host Which teams were these again?

Tom Indonesia and another South Korean pair.

Host So in both matches, the teams tried to lose instead of trying to win so they'd have a better chance of winning a medal. Is that right?

Tom Yes. That's exactly what happened. And it was really obvious, too – all the spectators started booing, it was so bad. After the second match, there was an investigation and all eight players were disqualified.

Host And what about the competition? Did it stop there?

Tom No, it continued without the disqualified players.

Host And who won the gold medal in the end?

Tom The first Chinese team. They beat the Japanese team in both sets. Actually, it was a very good match!

Host Tom, thanks for joining us.

Tom My pleasure.

5 B))

Host Hello, and welcome to the show. Now, a lot of research has been done recently about love, what causes it, and what we do to attract someone. Mary is in the studio with us today, and she's going to explain the results of some of these studies to us. Mary, welcome to the show.

Mary Hello.

Host Let's start with how to meet new people. Some people like to start a conversation with a person they like by saying something funny. But how useful is this?

Mary Not very useful at all I'm afraid, Jeremy. Research shows that only 7% of attraction has anything to do with what you say. It's the tone and the speed of your voice that make a difference.

This makes up 38% of the attraction. But the most important thing of all is body language. This contributes to a massive 55% of the attraction.

Host So what can we do to improve our body language?

Mary Well, it seems that the best way to make the person you're talking to feel attracted to you is to look into their eyes. An American psychologist did an experiment about this in New York. He got complete strangers to stare into each other's eyes for two minutes without talking. Afterward, many of the couples said that they had strong feelings of attraction to each other, and one of the couples even got married!

Host Really? Then staring must be the thing to do! Is there any more advice on body language?

Mary Well, it's important to have a relaxed body position. You need to show the other person that you're comfortable being with them. Also, try not to be far away from them. Of course, there is a comfortable distance, but try leaning a little closer to them than usual, it will show you're interested, and hold their attention better. Don't forget to watch their body language, too. If they position their body in a similar way to you, it means they find you interesting, too. This is called mirroring.

Host Is there anything that seems to work well when you're talking to someone you're attracted to?

Mary Not surprisingly, it seems that you'll have a better chance if you smile. Anyone who's ever spoken to someone on the phone will tell you that it's easy to tell when the other person is smiling, because you can hear it in their voice. When talking to a potential partner, a smile will not only affect your tone of voice, keeping it light and fun, but it will also show the other person that you are happy to be with them. And don't forget that a smile is extremely contagious, and before long the other person will be smiling back at you. This will make them feel happier, a feeling that they will quickly connect with you.

Host How interesting, and very true! Unfortunately, that's all we have time for now, Mary, but thank you so much for joining us.

Mary You're welcome.

6 A

Tour guide Hello, and welcome to the TV and Movie Walking Tour of Central Park in New York City. My name's Stacy Clinton, and I'm going to be your guide today. I hope you are all wearing comfortable shoes because the tour lasts for two hours. We'll end at Columbus Circle at around two o'clock.

We're going to start at Gapstow Bridge – a stone bridge originally built in 1874. From the bridge you have an amazing view of the Plaza Hotel. Does anyone know which movies the Plaza Hotel has been featured in? No? Well, you can see this famous hotel in *The Great Gatsby* and *Almost Famous* just to name two. So that's where we're going to go first. Then we're going to go to the Wollman Skating Rink—one of two rinks in the park. This skating rink was opened to the public in 1858, well over 150 years ago! You might recognize the rink from the movies *Home Alone 2* and *Love Story*.

After the rink, we'll walk to one of the most well-known attractions in Central Park—the Carousel. This carousel has 57 colorful wooden horses for children and adults to ride on, and it's only three dollars a ride! The original carousel was built in 1871. This one isn't the original, but it is beautiful. Maybe that's why director Mel Brooks chose to include it in his movie, *The Producers*.

As we walk toward the middle of the park, we'll pass by the Promenade and Bethesda Fountain where movies such as *The Avengers, Breakfast at Tiffany's,* and *Enchanted* shot scenes. Farther north, we'll take a look at the largest lake in Central Park and we'll visit the Boathouse Restaurant, which was featured in the movie *When Harry Met Sally*. Next, we'll visit the Bow Bridge—a graceful cast-iron bridge, which is considered one of the most romantic spots in New York City. Movie directors must agree because the bridge has been featured in *Spider-man 3,* on the TV show *Glee* and in one of the greatest love stories of all time—*The Way We Were*.

At this point, we'll visit Strawberry Fields, an area of the park dedicated to John Lennon and his music. We'll look at the beautiful memorial mosaic with the word "imagine" in the middle designed to honor Lennon's memory. Of course, this area of the park was also used for a scene in the movie *Little Manhattan*.

Finally, we'll walk to the Sheep Meadow. Don't worry—there haven't been any sheep in this meadow since 1934. However, we will see people sunbathing or relaxing in this 15-acre open area. This location was used in scenes for *Wall Street* and *The Fisher King*.

As we walk to our final destination, Columbus Circle, we'll pass by Tavern on the Green, once a famous restaurant in New York City and also used as a location for the popular movie *Ghostbusters*. And finally, we'll end up at Columbus Circle where scenes for *Taxi Driver* and *Borat* were shot. OK, so let's get going and head to our first stop, Gapstow Bridge…

6 B

Host Hello, and welcome to today's program. Have you ever wondered how women made themselves look beautiful in the past? Our beauty expert Olivia Johnson is with us today, and she's going to tell us all about beauty through the ages. Olivia, where are you going to start?

Olivia Well, I'm going to start with the Egyptians, but it wasn't only women who used cosmetics at this time. Both Egyptian men and women loved their cosmetics – we know that from the paintings and the powders they left behind. The women wore a powder on their faces to make their skin lighter, and they painted a big black line around their eyes to make them look bigger. Men put a cream made of fat and oil and other substances on their face to protect it from the sun – a very early version of sunscreen. Egyptian kings and queens also put colorful powders around their eyes. Their favorite color was green, which they got from a mineral called malachite.

Host How interesting! Who are you going to tell us about next?

Olivia OK! Let's move on to the ancient Greeks. Cosmetics were an important part of their life, too. The ancient Greek idea of beauty was very pale skin, blonde hair, and natural makeup. For them, pale skin was a sign of beauty and wealth. The women used a powder made out of a metal called lead to make their faces look lighter.

Host You mean lead? The lead that used to be in the pipes carrying the water in our houses?

Olivia That's right.

Host But lead is poisonous!

Olivia Yes, it is, and the ancient Greeks

knew lead was poisonous, but it was so important for them to be beautiful that they used it on their face, and of course, it made them sick.

Host I can't believe they used lead on their faces! Anyway, who's next on the list?

Olivia The Romans. They were absolutely obsessed with beauty. A Roman philosopher once wrote, "A woman without paint is like food without salt," so it's clear that they really believed that women should wear a lot of makeup. The Romans believed that pink on the cheeks was a sign of good health, but they did not apply the makeup themselves. Instead, they used their servants to put on their creams and powders.

Host So, the servants were like modern makeup artists, then?

Olivia Yes, I guess you could say that.

Host I think I prefer putting on my own makeup. Olivia Johnson, thank you for joining us.

Olivia My pleasure.

7 A))

Host And now for a review of last night's TV shows. The highlight for me was a new series called *The Unteachables*. It's a kind of reality show that tries to find out if it's really true that there are students who can't be taught. Last night, we were introduced to the students. There are 16 of them altogether, and they're all 14 years old. They've all been suspended from schools at least once, and their teachers think they're impossible to teach. Watching the students on last night's show, it isn't hard to see why. We see the group during their introductory weekend at the study camp when they meet each other for the first time. At one point, one of the boys warns that he might set the building on fire. You couldn't imagine how their teacher was going to teach them.

And that's where 40-year old Philip Beadle comes in. Beadle used to be a rock musician, but he gave up music at the age of 32 to become a teacher. Since then, he has had a very successful career in education. His greatest achievement was when he worked at a high school where there were a lot of problems. He worked really hard, and his students got the best test scores in English that the school had ever seen – all of his students passed their exams, half of them with the highest score. But let me get back to the show.

In Beadle's first class, he manages to help the students learn to trust him by playing a game with the children. In the game, Beadle and the students point at each other and say an insult. This might not seem very educational, but Beadle had the attention of all the students, and everybody was joining in. And that was the point of the game.

You might think that Beadle's teaching methods are pretty unusual, and you'd be right. At one point on last night's show, he took the students out into the country. They found a field with cows in it, and he made them read poems and plays by Shakespeare to the cows! Remember that these are children who refuse to read in front of other people in a classroom. In another scene, they are in a different field, learning about punctuation. Beadle teaches this by going around to different students and shouting the names of the types of punctuation. So, for example he shouts "question mark," then "huh!" and at the same time moves his body into a shape like a question mark. The students learn by copying him, and it looks like a lot of fun. By the end of the first episode, the students are starting to accept their new teacher. Some of them even say he's "all right."

I really enjoyed *The Unteachables* and I really want to know what happens next. If you're fascinated by the experiment like I am, you'll watch the next episode at the same time next Wednesday. Personally, I can't wait!

7 B))

Guide: Ladies and gentlemen, can I have your attention, please? Thank you and welcome to Graceland, the home of music star Elvis Presley. We start our tour here, at the front door of this impressive home. This is the perfect place to look closely at the outside of the house. It was built in the early part of the twentieth century, in a style that was popular at the time. The outside walls of the house are made of stone and wood, and the house has two floors as well as a basement. This house was Elvis's home from 1957 until 1977 when he died, which means he spent most of his adulthood here. He got married in 1967 and his wife, Priscilla, came to live with him here after they got married. Their only daughter Lisa Marie was born here. So you see, this house played an extremely important role in Elvis's life. Now, as you're walking through the house, I'd like you to pay special attention to how different rooms are decorated. One room is decorated to look like a jungle with green rugs, plants of all kinds, and animal-print decorations. Another room, the TV room, was one of the first "home theaters" in the US. Elvis placed three TVs side-by-side on a wall. On Sundays, he could watch three different football games at the same time! OK, if you'll come this way, we'll start on the first floor, and the first room we're going to visit is the dining room.

Are you all in? Well, this is the dining room where Elvis enjoyed meals with his guests. The large dining room table could seat about 12 people. The beautiful light hanging over the table is made of Italian glass. Elvis didn't usually wake up until four in the afternoon, so the dinner parties didn't start until ten at night! His full-time cooks made old-fashioned Southern food for the dinner parties – and when he wanted a snack, his cooks made him his favorite peanut butter, banana, and bacon sandwiches…which were probably the reason he gained weight as he got older! The dining room was also used by Elvis as a place to play card games with his friends.

Now, we're going to walk across the hall to the living room, and then we'll head to the music room right behind it. Please follow me.

The centerpiece of the living room is a 14-foot-long white leather couch and 10-foot-long coffee table. Quite impressive! The room has a wall covered in mirrors and is decorated in gold, blue, and white. If you look over here, you'll see a pair of stained-glass birds that lead into the music room. It was in this room that Elvis and his friends spent hours together creating and playing music. When you're ready, we'll continue with our tour of the first floor and visit the kitchen and Elvis's parents' room, where his father had a swimming pool installed in his bedroom along with a jukebox next to it!

8 A))

Laura Hi, Sam! How was your trip to Chicago?

Sam It was great, thanks. But the flight back was awful! In fact, I made a complaint to the airline.

Laura What was the problem?

Sam Well, as you know, some airlines make you wait forever in line before you can board, which I can't stand. It also means that there's always a huge rush to get on the plane and there isn't any place to put your bags. I find all this so annoying that I usually pay for PreferredAccess – you know, when you pay extra to get on the plane first. You just get in line when they call the flight, and then they tell the passengers with PreferredAccess to come to the front and you get on the plane first.

Laura So what went wrong?

Sam Well, it was fine on the flight to Chicago. I stood in line, they called the people who had PreferredAccess, I boarded the plane, and I got to my seat with no problems. Perfect! But on the flight back from Chicago to New York, I was standing in line at the gate waiting to be called to board first, and nothing happened. I don't know if they forgot about PreferredAccess or what, but they didn't call us to the front of the line. That meant I had to board the plane with everyone else – in fact, I was one of the last to get on. As you can imagine, I wasn't very happy.

Laura So, what did you do?

Sam When I got home, I emailed the airline explaining what had happened. I told them that I had paid for PreferredAccess on both of my flights, but I had only received the service on one of them. I asked them, very politely, to give back the money I had paid for the PreferredAccess for the return trip. It was about $20 at the time.

Laura Did you get a response?

Sam Yes, I did. They were very quick. I sent my email at 5 p.m., and I received a reply the next morning.

Laura And did they give you your money back?

Sam Well, no, they didn't. I had a very nice message from a man in customer service saying he was concerned about the incident. But he didn't say he would give me my money back.

Laura Typical! They never do, do they?

Sam Wait a minute – I haven't finished the story yet.

Laura Oh. Sorry…go ahead.

Sam Well, I sent them a second email. But this time the tone was much stronger and less polite. And it worked! They refunded my PreferredAccess AND they gave me money for my return flight from Chicago. I was impressed!

Laura That's great!

8 B))

Speaker 1 When I was about 15, I got a part-time job in a supermarket. The job was in the cash office, so I had a lot of responsibility. I had to collect the money from the registers, count it, and put it in the safe for the security people to collect the next morning. I was still in school at the time, so I worked for a couple of hours on a Friday evening and all day on Saturdays. During the holidays I worked more hours because I had more time and there were more customers. The girls in the office were a lot of fun, so the job wasn't at all boring. I worked there for about three years, until I left because I needed more time to study for my final exams at school.

Speaker 2 I studied Spanish in college and at the end of my first year, I went to Argentina to practice my Spanish. I found a job in a restaurant almost as soon as I arrived. The job was washing dishes, which I thought was going to be easy. Unfortunately, I was wrong. There was a machine in the kitchen that washed the plates and glasses and things like that. But my job was to clean the pots and pans that the chef had used. The saucepans were always completely black and it used to take me hours to get everything clean. I didn't enjoy working there very much, and I was really happy when I had learned enough Spanish so that I could stop working there.

Speaker 3 I don't know if you can call this a job, but I did get paid for it, even if it was only twenty dollars! When I was a teenager, I used to take care of my cousins when my aunt and uncle wanted to go out. The kids were a lot younger than me, so I had to babysit for them. I didn't do it every weekend, but it was probably about once a month. My uncle used to pick me up at about seven and take me back to their house. I had to bathe the kids, give them their dinner, and play with them for an hour or so before they went to bed. They were no trouble at all to babysit, and I absolutely loved being with them!

Speaker 4 My dad's a painter, and so the summer after I finished school, I went to help him for a few weeks. At the time, my dad's company had a contract to paint all the exterior doors and windows of some houses in a new development. The weather was great – not too hot and not too cold, so I didn't really mind it. The work was pretty tiring because I spent most of the day climbing up and down a ladder, but I earned a lot of money that summer. But the best thing was spending some time with my dad and his colleagues– we had a really good time!

Speaker 5 One of the first jobs I ever had was in a food processing company in San Diego. I was a student at the time, and I needed a temporary job during the holidays. Fortunately, the job was only for two weeks because it was really awful. The worst day was when we were packaging hamburgers. I had to stand on the production line and count the burgers into groups of five. Later, someone farther down the line put the burgers in a box. The problem was that the burgers were frozen and we weren't allowed to wear gloves. This meant that I had to pick up the ice-cold burgers with my hands. I've never had such cold fingers in all my life!

9 A))

Speaker 1 I know a lot of people who are superstitious when they see somebody standing on top of a ladder on the sidewalk and they don't want to walk underneath it. Actually, I'm one of those people! Walking under a ladder is supposed to give you bad luck, so I never do it. Whenever I come across a ladder, I always walk around it – even if I have to walk out into the street. Come to think of it, that's probably worse than walking under the ladder because I could get hit by a car, but there's no way that I would ever walk under the ladder.

Speaker 2 I don't know if any other countries have this superstition, but where I live, you have to be very careful when you buy a new pair of shoes. Apparently, it's bad luck to put the shoes on your dining room table. This goes back to something that people did in the past when somebody died – in fact, it was the families of miners in the north of England who originally did this. The family always bought new clothes to dress the dead person in, and this included buying new shoes. So, if you leave your new shoes on the table, some people think that this could bring bad luck.

Speaker 3 In some countries, some people are very superstitious about going up or down stairs. If you're going down stairs, it's bad luck to pass someone who's coming up the stairs and the same thing happens the other way around. Someone once told me the reason for this. A long time ago, people carried swords so you had to be very careful of the people around you. If somebody passed you on the stairs you couldn't see them because they were behind you. That meant that they could turn around and kill you with their sword without you realizing.

Speaker 4 When I was planning my wedding a couple of years ago, I had my heart set on a beautiful outdoor spring ceremony in November. Unfortunately, my husband's brother was engaged at the same time, and in Chile it's considered bad luck for two brothers to get married during the same year. Since his brother is the eldest, he got to choose his wedding date first. Of course he chose November. We had to wait until January, in the middle of summer. Our wedding day was one of the hottest days of the year! It was so uncomfortable in my dress and my hair was out of control!

Speaker 5 In Brazil, if someone has an exam or is going for a job interview, we push our thumb between our first two fingers to wish them luck. I have some German friends who make a similar sign. They wrap the fingers of their right hand around their thumb and say, "I'm holding my thumb for you." And I know that in the US people cross their fingers and say "fingers crossed" when they wish people luck, which is also similar. Maybe they're all connected in some way.

9 B))

Receptionist Good afternoon. Can I help you?
Guest Oh, hello. Yes – I need to ask you about Wi-Fi access in the hotel. I have some work to do while I'm here, so I'm going to need an Internet connection.
Receptionist Well, there's a Wi-Fi hotspot in the lobby of the hotel and all of the rooms have Wi-Fi.
Guest Great. And how much does it cost?
Receptionist It's free in the lobby, but we charge for the Wi-Fi access in the rooms. Are you interested in our standard connection or would you prefer our advanced service?
Guest Um, what's the difference?
Receptionist The standard service is available for a flat fee of ten dollars per day. However, it can be a little bit slow because everyone in the hotel uses it. We have a higher-level service for our guests who need a faster and more reliable connection.
Guest And how much is that?
Receptionist It's 25 cents per minute.
Guest That could get pretty expensive if I use it all evening.
Receptionist Not really, Sir. The maximum charge is 30 dollars for 24 hours.
Guest I see. So how would that work? Would I have to pay 30 dollars today and another 30 dollars tomorrow?
Receptionist No. The 24-hour period begins from when you checked in.
Guest Great! I'd like the advanced service, then. Oh, and one more question. What do I need to log on to your Wi-Fi?
Receptionist Just a moment. Could you give me your name and room number?
Guest It's Gray. Barry Gray. I'm in room 302.
Receptionist Thank you, Mr. Gray. Here's your Wi-Fi pack, which has the name of the connection…here, and… here's your password. Please try to keep it safe so that nobody else can use it. You checked in at ten after three today, so the connection will last until the same time tomorrow afternoon.
Guest Great. Is that all I need?
Receptionist Yes, it is.
Guest Thanks a lot for your help.
Receptionist You're welcome.

10 A))

Host Welcome back to the show. Now, a new exhibition opens today at the Science Museum, and all of the exhibits are everyday objects that we couldn't live without. Charlotte Heath, who has been to the exhibition, is with us today to tell us more about it. Welcome to the show, Charlotte.
Charlotte Thank you.
Host So what kinds of objects can you see in the exhibition? Are we talking about modern gadgets like smartphones and tablets here?
Charlotte No, no, not at all. This exhibition is all about the little or important things we have in our house and use every day. We use them so much that we probably forgot, or don't even realize, that someone actually invented them.
Host Such as?
Charlotte Well, a good example is the container we use to keep food in: the tin can. But I bet you don't know how it was invented.
Host No, I don't.
Charlotte Well, there's a very interesting story behind it. It was the French leader Napoleon Bonaparte who was responsible for this one. In 1809, he was worried about how to feed all his soldiers when they were away from home, so he organized a competition to try to get ideas for how to solve the problem. The first prize was 12,000 Francs and the competition was won by a French chef who had the idea of using glass jars to store food. A year later, a British manufacturer, Peter Durand, improved the design by using thin sheets of metal to make the container that became what we now call a tin can. The only problem was that he used lead in the can, which as you know is poisonous. Several people died after eating food from his tin cans.
Host How unfortunate! Now, Charlotte, do we have time for one more story before the news headlines?
Charlotte Sure. I can tell you about the tea bag. In the past, if you wanted to buy tea, you had to buy the leaves in a big box. To make a drink of tea, you would put the leaves in water, and you would often find small pieces of tea leaves at the bottom of your cup. Anyway, in 1908, an American tea salesperson named Thomas Sullivan had the bright idea of putting the tea in very small bags to give to his customers to try. Sullivan thought that customers would take the tea out of the bags in order to try it, but some of the customers didn't. They found it more convenient to put the bag into hot water, without actually opening it. So, tea bags weren't really invented by a company, it was the tea drinkers who came up with the idea!
Host What an incredible story! And the Everyday Inventions Exhibition at the Science Museum will run until Sunday, July 25th. Right, Charlotte?
Charlotte Yes. The museum is open from ten to six every day, so there's no excuse not to go.
Host Thanks for joining us, Charlotte. And now it's time for the news headlines with…

10 B))

The next morning when my servant Paddock arrived, I introduced him to Captain Digby. I explained that the

Captain was an important man in the army, but he had been working too hard and needed rest and quiet. Then I went out, leaving them both in the flat. When I returned about lunchtime, the doorman told me that the gentleman in flat 15 had killed himself. I went up to the top floor, had a few words with the police, and was able to report to Scudder that his plan had been successful. The police believed that the dead man was Scudder, and that he had killed himself. Scudder was very pleased.

For the first two days in my flat, he was very calm, and spent all his time reading and smoking, and writing in a little black notebook. But after that he became more restless and nervous. It was not his own danger that he worried about, but the success of his plan to prevent the murder of Karolides. One night he was very serious.

"Listen, Hannay," he said. "I think I must tell you some more about this business. I would hate to get killed without leaving someone else to carry on with my plan."

I didn't listen very carefully. I was interested in Scudder's adventures, but I wasn't very interested in politics. I remember that he said Karolides was only in danger in London. He also mentioned a woman called Julia Czechenyi.

The next evening I had to go out. I was meeting a man I had known in Africa for dinner. When I returned to the flat, I was surprised to see that the study light was out. I wondered if Scudder had gone to bed early. I turned on the light, but there was nobody there. Then I saw something in the corner that made my blood turn cold.

Scudder was lying on his back. There was a long knife through his heart, pinning him to the floor.

198 Madison Avenue
New York, NY 10016 USA

Great Clarendon Street, Oxford, OX2 6DP, United Kingdom

Oxford University Press is a department of the University of Oxford. It furthers the University's objective of excellence in research, scholarship, and education by publishing worldwide. Oxford is a registered trade mark of Oxford University Press in the UK and in certain other countries

© Oxford University Press 2014

The moral rights of the author have been asserted

First published in 2014

2023 2022 2021 2020

16 15 14 13 12 11

No unauthorized photocopying

All rights reserved. No part of this publication may be reproduced, stored in a retrieval system, or transmitted, in any form or by any means, without the prior permission in writing of Oxford University Press, or as expressly permitted by law, by licence or under terms agreed with the appropriate reprographics rights organization. Enquiries concerning reproduction outside the scope of the above should be sent to the ELT Rights Department, Oxford University Press, at the address above

You must not circulate this work in any other form and you must impose this same condition on any acquirer

Links to third party websites are provided by Oxford in good faith and for information only. Oxford disclaims any responsibility for the materials contained in any third party website referenced in this work

ISBN: 978 0 19 477605 9 WORKBOOK

Printed in China

This book is printed on paper from certified and well-managed sources

ACKNOWLEDGEMENTS

The authors and publisher are grateful to those who have given permission to reproduce the following extracts and adaptations of copyright material:

p.19 Extract from http://www.roughguides.com/article/10-unusual-types-oftransport/. Copyright © 2013 ROUGH GUIDES LTD. Reproduced by permission of Rough Guides Ltd.; p.47 Extract from 'Why houses with history will sell' by Christopher Middleton, The Telegraph, 20 June 2011. © Telegraph Media Group Limited 2011. Reproduced by permission; p.51 Extract from 'Ten tips for safe shopping online this Christmas' by Stephen Ellis, The Telegraph, 8 December 2008. © Telegraph Media Group Limited 2008. Reproduced by permission; p.57 Extract from 'Lucky it wasn't raining! Moment driver was catapulted through sunroof of flipping car…and walked away unharmed' by Emma Reynolds, The Daily Mail, 10 July 2012. Reproduced by permission of Solo Syndication; p.61 Extract from 'What to do when you spill a drink on your laptop' by Jack Schofield, The Guardian, 5 July 2012. Copyright Guardian News & Media Ltd 2012. Reproduced by permission; p.64 Extract from 'This much I know: Usain Bolt' by Mark Bailey, The Guardian, 17 June 2012. Copyright Guardian News & Media Ltd 2012. Reproduced by permission; p.67 Extract from 'Oxford Bookworms Library: The Thirty-Nine Steps' by John Buchan, retold by Nick Bullard, Series Editor Jennifer Bassett. © Oxford University Press 2007. Reprinted by permission; p.23 Extract from www.newyorktaxis.org. Reproduced by permission; p.62 Extract from Slate, © 12 November 2008 Issue, The Slate Group All rights reserved. Used by permission and protected by the Copyright Laws of the United States. The printing, copying, redistribution, or retransmission of the Material without express written permission is prohibited; p.36 Extract from 'USA Getting there & around', www.lonelyplanet.com. Reproduced with permission from the Lonely Planet website www.lonelyplanet.com © 2012 Lonely Planet.

Illustrations by: Satoshi Hashimoto/Dutch Uncle: pp.14, 57; Anna Hymas/New Division: p.20; Tim Marrs: p.13; Jerome Mireault/Colagene: pp.28, 40; Ellis Nadler: pronunciation symbols; Roger Penwill: p.59; Ron Tiner: pp.67, 68; Kath Walker: p.41.

We would also like to thank the following for permission to reproduce the following photographs:
Cover: Gemenacom/shutterstock.com, Andrey_Popov/shutterstock.com, Wavebreakmedia/shutterstock.com, Image Source/Getty Images, Lane Oatey/Blue Jean Images/Getty Images, BJI/Blue Jean Images/Getty Images, Image Source/Corbis, Yuri Arcurs/Tetra Images/Corbis, Wavebreak Media Ltd./Corbis; pg.4 (2 across) studiomode/Alamy, (3 across) Gastromedia/Alamy, (5 across) Food and Drink Photos/Alamy, (1 down) Annabelle Breakey/Getty Images, (2 down) Dave King/Getty Images, (4 down) jon whitaker/Getty Images; pg.6 Mike Kemp/Tetra Images/Corbis; pg.7 (1) Sean Justice/Getty Images, (2) Image Source/Corbis, (3) JGI/Getty Images, (4) PhotoAlto/Eric Audras/Getty Images, (5) Jose Luis Pelaez Inc/Getty Images; pg.9 Stefano Ravera/Alamy; pg.10 Brian Hamill/Getty Images; pg.11 2020WEB/Alamy; pg.15 (bus) Thomas Cockrem/Alamy, (construction) Ryan Smith/Somos Images/Corbis, (orangutan) Andrew Watson/Getty Images; pg.16 (1) Lobke Peers/shutterstock, (2) LJSphotography/Alamy, (3) Rich Legg/Getty Images, (4) John Rowley/Getty Images, (5) Denis Scott/Corbis, (6) Everynight Images/Alamy; pg.18 (China) Ma Hailin/Xinhua Press/Corbis, (Mexico) Danny Lehman/Corbis, (Australia) John Gollings/Arcaid/Corbis; pg.19 (boat) Julia Rogers/Alamy, (sled) Accent Alaska.com/Alamy, (train) STRINGER/CAMBODIA/X80007/Reuters/Corbis, (jeep) Christian Kober/Robert Harding World Imagery/Corbis; pg.22 (man) Ann Summa/Corbis, (woman) Flashon Studio/shutterstock; pg.23 Bufflerump/shutterstock.com; pg.24 Erik Isakson/Blend Images/Corbis; pg.25 (Speilberg) Luc Roux/Sygma/Corbis, (Newton) The Gallery Collection/Corbis, (Gates) Peer Grimm/dpa/Corbis, (Edison) CORBIS; pg.27 (Liberty) Rubens Alarcon/shutterstock, (Times Square) Kobby Dagan/shutterstock.com; pg.32 Michael Regan/Getty Images; pg.34 (friends) Dreampictures/Image Source/Corbis, (couple) Monkey Business Images/shutterstock; pg.36 Car Culture/Getty Images; pg.38 (Knebworth House) Steven Vidler/Eurasia Press/Corbis, (Anna Karenina) 2012/Moviestore/Rex; pg.39 (carousel) Ambient Images Inc./Alamy, (table) Anna Clopet/CORBIS, (rink) Kiet Thai/Getty Images, (bridge) Andrew C Mace/Getty Images; pg.42 Dimitri Otis/Getty Images; pg.44 Ken Seet/Corbis; pg.45 epa european pressphoto agency b.v./Alamy; pg.47 (Graceland) Jon Arnold Images Ltd/Alamy, (cabin) jpbcpa/istock, (apartment) cdrin/shutterstock.com; pg.48 Jeff Morgan 12/Alamy; pg.51 auremar/shutterstock; pg.52 Mira Oberman/AFP/Getty Images; pg.53 Blend Images/shutterstock; pg.54 C. Devan/Corbis; pg.55 (dentist) Julian Abram Wainwright/epa/Corbis, (golf) Andrew Geiger/Getty Images; pg.57 Top-Pics TBK/Alamy; pg.58 Mathew Crowcoot/Newsteam/SWNS Group; pg.59 Tokyo Space Club/Corbis; pg.60 (keyboard) S.E.A. Photo/Alamy, (plug) Carsten Reisinger/Alamy, (outlet) Joe Belanger/shutterstock, (switch) Olivier Le Queinec/shutterstock, (headphones) Bryan Solomon/shutterstock, (USB) cristi180884/shutterstock, (speaker) arigato/shutterstock, (mouse) vasabii/shutterstock, (screen) yanugkelid/shutterstock, (remote) MNI/shutterstock, (flashdrive) bogdan ionescu/shutterstock, (adaptor) Freer/shutterstock; pg.61 R and R Images/Getty Images; pg.63 (Selena) AP Photo/Blanca Charolet, Premier Postage via Hispanic PR Wire, HO, (Jay Z) Ben Rowland/The Hell Gate/Corbis, (bridge) Imaginechina/Corbis, (Kyi) Anindito Mukherjee/epa/Corbis, (Craig) EON/DANJAQ/SONY/The Kobal Collection/Maidment, Jay, (Mesa Verde) MarclSchauer/shutterstock, (Louvre) Migel/shutterstock.com, (Everest) Pal Teravagimov/shutterstock; pg.64 (1) NetPhotos/Alamy, (2) leolintang/shutterstock, (3) Alexander Demyanenko/shutterstock, (4) Erkan Mehmet/Alamy, (5) Asianet-Pakistan/shutterstock.com, (6) Bernd Kohlhas/Corbis, (7) Ferenc Szelepcsenyi/shutterstock, (8) claudiodivizia/istock, (Bolt) Christopher Morris/Corbis; pg.65 (1) pockygallery/shutterstock, (2) Burdika/shutterstock, (3) Graphic design/shutterstock, (4) anaken2012/shutterstock, (5) Anton Prado PHOTO/shutterstock, (6) maniacpixel/shutterstock; pg.66 Arthur Turner/Alamy.